THE THEORY OF THE THEATRE

AND OTHER PRINCIPLES OF DRAMATIC CRITICISM

BY

CLAYTON HAMILTON

AUTHOR OF "MATERIALS AND METHODS OF FICTION"

NEW YORK
HENRY HOLT AND COMPANY
1913

TO

BRANDER MATTHEWS

MENTOR AND FRIEND
WHO FIRST AWAKENED MY CRITICAL INTEREST
IN THE THEORY OF THE THEATRE

PREFACE

Most of the chapters which make up the present volume have already appeared, in earlier versions, in certain magazines; and to the editors of *The Forum, The North American Review, The Smart Set,* and *The Bookman,* I am indebted for permission to republish such materials as I have culled from my contributions to their pages. Though these papers were written at different times and for different immediate circles of subscribers, they were all designed from the outset to illustrate certain steady central principles of dramatic criticism; and, thus collected, they afford, I think, a consistent exposition of the most important points in the theory of the theatre. The introductory chapter, entitled *What is a Play?*, has not, in any form, appeared in print before; and all the other papers have been diligently revised, and in many passages entirely rewritten.

C. H.

New York City: 1910.

CONTENTS

THE THEORY OF THE THEATRE

OTHER PRINCIPLES OF DRAMATIC CRITICISM

THE THEORY OF THE THEATRE

THE
THEORY OF THE THEATRE

I

WHAT IS A PLAY?

A PLAY is a story devised to be presented by
actors on a stage before an audience.

This plain statement of fact affords an exceedingly simple definition of the drama,— a definition
so simple indeed as to seem at the first glance easily
obvious and therefore scarcely worthy of expression. But if we examine the statement thoroughly,
phrase by phrase, we shall see that it sums up
within itself the entire theory of the theatre, and
that from this primary axiom we may deduce the
whole practical philosophy of dramatic criticism.

It is unnecessary to linger long over an explanation of the word " story." A story is a representation of a series of events linked together by
the law of cause and effect and marching forward
toward a predestined culmination,— each event exhibiting imagined characters performing imagined
acts in an appropriate imagined setting. This

definition applies, of course, to the epic, the ballad, the novel, the short-story, and all other forms of narrative art, as well as to the drama.

But the phrase " devised to be presented " distinguishes the drama sharply from all other forms of narrative. In particular it must be noted that a play is not a story that is written to be read. By no means must the drama be considered primarily as a department of literature,— like the epic or the novel, for example. Rather, from the standpoint of the theatre, should literature be considered as only one of a multitude of means which the dramatist must employ to convey his story effectively to the audience. The great Greek dramatists needed a sense of sculpture as well as a sense of poetry; and in the contemporary theatre the playwright must manifest the imagination of the painter as well as the imagination of the man of letters. The appeal of a play is primarily visual rather than auditory. On the contemporary stage, characters properly costumed must be exhibited within a carefully designed and painted setting illuminated with appropriate effects of light and shadow; and the art of music is often called upon to render incidental aid to the general impression. The dramatist, therefore, must be endowed not only with the literary sense, but also with a clear eye for the graphic and plastic elements of pictorial effect, a sense of rhythm and of music, and a thorough knowledge of the art of acting. Since the dramatist must, at the same time and in the same work, harness and harmonise the methods of so many of the arts, it would be uncritical to centre studious consideration solely on his dialogue and to praise him or condemn him on the literary ground alone.

It is, of course, true that the very greatest plays have always been great literature as well as great drama. The purely literary element — the final touch of style in dialogue — is the only sure antidote against the opium of time. Now that Æschylus is no longer performed as a playwright, we read him as a poet. But, on the other hand, we should remember that the main reason why he is no longer played is that his dramas do not fit the modern theatre,— an edifice totally different in size and shape and physical appointments from that in which his pieces were devised to be presented. In his own day he was not so much read as a poet as applauded in the theatre as a playwright; and properly to appreciate his dramatic, rather than his literary, appeal, we must reconstruct in our imagination the conditions of the theatre in his day. The point is that his plays, though planned primarily as drama, have since been shifted over, by many generations of critics and literary students, into the adjacent province of poetry; and this shift of the critical point of view, which has insured the immortality of Æschylus, has been made possible only by the literary merit of his dialogue. When a play, owing to altered physical conditions, is tossed out of the theatre, it will find a haven in the closet only if it be greatly written. From this fact we may derive the practical maxim that though a skilful playwright need not write greatly in order to secure the plaudits of his own generation, he must cultivate a literary excellence if he wishes to be remembered by posterity.

This much must be admitted concerning the ultimate importance of the literary element in the drama. But on the other hand it must be granted that many plays that stand very high as drama do not fall within the range of literature. A typical example is the famous melodrama by Dennery entitled *The Two Orphans*. This play has deservedly held the stage for nearly a century, and bids fair still to be applauded after the youngest critic has died. It is undeniably a very good play. It tells a thrilling story in a series of carefully graded theatric situations. It presents nearly a dozen acting parts which, though scarcely real as characters, are yet drawn with sufficient fidelity to fact to allow the performers to produce a striking illusion of reality during the two hours' traffic of the stage. It is, to be sure — especially in the standard English translation — abominably written. One of the two orphans launches wide-

eyed upon a soliloquy beginning, "Am I mad?
. . . Do I dream?"; and such sentences as the
following obtrude themselves upon the astounded
ear,—"If you persist in persecuting me in this
heartless manner, I shall inform the police."
Nothing, surely, could be further from literature.
Yet thrill after thrill is conveyed, by visual means,
through situations artfully contrived; and in the
sheer excitement of the moment, the audience is
made incapable of noticing the pompous mediocrity
of the lines.

In general, it should be frankly understood by
students of the theatre that an audience is not capable of hearing whether the dialogue of a play is
well or badly written. Such a critical discrimina-
tion would require an extraordinary nicety of ear,
and might easily be led astray, in one direction or
the other, by the reading of the actors. The
rhetoric of Massinger must have sounded like
poetry to an Elizabethan audience that had heard
the same performers, the afternoon before, speaking lines of Shakespeare's. If Mr. Forbes-Robertson is reading a poorly-written part, it is hard
to hear that the lines are, in themselves, not musical. Literary style is, even for accomplished critics, very difficult to judge in the theatre. Some
years ago, Mrs. Fiske presented in New York an
English adaptation of Paul Heyse's *Mary of Magdala*. After the first performance — at which I

did not happen to be present — I asked several cultivated people who had heard the play whether the English version was written in verse or in prose; and though these people were themselves actors and men of letters, not one of them could tell me. Yet, as appeared later, when the play was published, the English dialogue was written in blank verse by no less a poet than Mr. William Winter. If such an elementary distinction as that between verse and prose was in this case inaudible to cultivated ears, how much harder must it be for the average audience to distinguish between a good phrase and a bad! The fact is that literary style is, for the most part, wasted on an audience. The average auditor is moved mainly by the emotional content of a sentence spoken on the stage, and pays very little attention to the form of words in which the meaning is set forth. At Hamlet's line, "Absent thee from felicity a while"— which Matthew Arnold, with impeccable taste, selected as one of his touchstones of literary style — the thing that really moves the audience in the theatre is not the perfectness of the phrase but the pathos of Hamlet's plea for his best friend to outlive him and explain his motives to a world grown harsh.

That the content rather than the literary turn of dialogue is the thing that counts most in the theatre will be felt emphatically if we compare the mere writing of Molière with that of his successor and imitator, Regnard. Molière is certainly a great writer, in the sense that he expresses clearly and precisely the thing he has to say; his verse, as well as his prose, is admirably lucid and eminently speakable. But assuredly, in the sense in which the word is generally used, Molière is not a poet; and it may fairly be said that, in the usual connotation of the term, he has no style. Regnard, on the other hand, is more nearly a poet, and, from the standpoint of style, writes vastly better verse. He has a lilting fluency that flowers every now and then into a phrase of golden melody. Yet Molière is so immeasurably his superior as a playwright that most critics instinctively set Regnard far below him even as a writer. There can be no question that M. Rostand writes better verse than Emile Augier; but there can be no question, also, that Augier is the greater dramatist. Oscar Wilde probably wrote more clever and witty lines than any other author in the whole history of English comedy; but no one would think of setting him in the class with Congreve and Sheridan.

It is by no means my intention to suggest that great writing is not desirable in the drama; but the point must be emphasised that it is not a necessary element in the immediate merit of a play *as a play*. In fact, excellent plays have often been presented without the use of any words at all.

Pantomime has, in every age, been recognised as a legitimate department of the drama. Only a few years ago, Mme. Charlotte Wiehe acted in New York a one-act play, entitled *La Main*, which held the attention enthralled for forty-five minutes during which no word was spoken. The little piece told a thrilling story with entire clearness and coherence, and exhibited three characters fully and distinctly drawn; and it secured this achievement by visual means alone, with no recourse whatever to the spoken word. Here was a work which by no stretch of terminology could have been included in the category of literature; and yet it was a very good play, and *as drama* was far superior to many a literary masterpiece in dialogue like Browning's *In a Balcony*.

Lest this instance seem too exceptional to be taken as representative, let us remember that throughout an entire important period in the history of the stage, it was customary for the actors to improvise the lines that they spoke before the audience. I refer to the period of the so-called *commedia dell'arte*, which flourished all over Italy throughout the sixteenth century. A synopsis of the play — partly narrative and partly expository — was posted up behind the scenes. This account of what was to happen on the stage was known technically as a *scenario*. The actors consulted this scenario before they made an entrance, and then in the acting of the scene spoke whatever words occurred to them. Harlequin made love to Columbine and quarreled with Pantaloon in new lines every night; and the drama gained both spontaneity and freshness from the fact that it was created anew at each performance. Undoubtedly, if an actor scored with a clever line, he would remember it for use in a subsequent presentation; and in this way the dialogue of a comedy must have gradually become more or less fixed and, in a sense, written. But this secondary task of formulating the dialogue was left to the performers; and the playwright contented himself with the primary task of planning the plot.

The case of the *commedia dell'arte* is, of course, extreme; but it emphasises the fact that the problem of the dramatist is less a task of writing than a task of constructing. His primary concern is so to build a story that it will tell itself to the eye of the audience in a series of shifting pictures. Any really good play can, to a great extent, be appreciated even though it be acted in a foreign language. American students in New York may find in the Yiddish dramas of the Bowery an emphatic illustration of how closely a piece may be followed by an auditor who does not understand the words of a single line. The recent extraordinary development in the art of the moving picture, especially in France, has taught us that many well-known plays may be presented in pantomime and reproduced by the kinetoscope, with no essential loss of intelligibility through the suppression of the dialogue. Sardou, as represented by the biograph, is no longer a man of letters; but he remains, scarcely less evidently than in the ordinary theatre, a skilful and effective playwright. *Hamlet*, that masterpiece of meditative poetry, would still be a good play if it were shown in moving pictures. Much, of course, would be sacrificed through the subversion of its literary element; but its essential interest *as a play* would yet remain apparent through the unassisted power of its visual appeal.

There can be no question that, however important may be the dialogue of a drama, the scenario is even more important; and from a full scenario alone, before a line of dialogue is written, it is possible in most cases to determine whether a prospective play is inherently good or bad. Most contemporary dramatists, therefore, postpone the actual writing of their dialogue until they have worked out their scenario in minute detail. They begin by separating and grouping their narrative materials into not more than three or four distinct pigeon-holes of time and place,— thereby dividing their story roughly into acts. They then plan a stage-setting for each act, employing whatever accessories may be necessary for the action. If papers are to be burned, they introduce a fire-place; if somebody is to throw a pistol through a window, they set the window in a convenient and emphatic place; they determine how many chairs and tables and settees are demanded for the narrative; if a piano or a bed is needed, they place it here or there upon the floor-plan of their stage, according to the prominence they wish to give it; and when all such points as these have been determined, they draw a detailed map of the stage-setting for the act. As their next step, most playwrights, with this map before them, and using a set of chess-men or other convenient concrete objects to represent their characters, move the pieces about upon the stage through the successive scenes, determine in detail where every character is to stand or sit at nearly every moment, and note down what he is to think and feel and talk about at the time. Only after the entire play has been planned out thus minutely does the average playwright turn back to the beginning and commence to write his dialogue. He completes his primary task of play-making before he begins his secondary task of play-writing. Many of our established dramatists — like the late Clyde Fitch, for example — sell their plays when the scenario is finished, arrange for the production, select the actors, and afterwards write the dialogue with the chosen actors constantly in mind.

This summary statement of the usual process may seem, perhaps, to cast excessive emphasis on the constructive phase of the playwright's problem; and allowance must of course be made for the divergent mental habits of individual authors. But almost any playwright will tell you that he feels as if his task were practically finished when he arrives at the point when he finds himself prepared to begin the writing of his dialogue. This accounts for the otherwise unaccountable rapidity with which many of the great plays of the world have been written. Dumas *fils* retired to the country and wrote *La Dame aux Camélias* — a four-act play — in eight successive days. But he had previously told the same story in a novel; he knew everything that was to happen in his play; and the mere writing could be done in a single headlong dash. Voltaire's best tragedy, *Zaïre*, was written in three weeks. Victor Hugo composed *Marion Delorme* between June 1 and June 24, 1829; and when the piece was interdicted by the censor, he immediately turned to another subject and wrote *Hernani* in the next three weeks. The fourth act of *Marion Delorme* was written in a single day. Here apparently was a very fever of composition. But again we must remember that both of these plays had been devised before the author began to write them; and when he took his pen in hand he had already been working on them in scenario for probably a year. To write ten acts in Alexandrines, with feminine rhymes alternating with masculine, was still, to be sure, an appalling task; but Hugo was a facile and prolific poet, and could write very quickly after he had determined exactly what it was he had to write.

It was with all of the foregoing points in mind that, in the opening sentence of this chapter, I defined a play as a story "devised," rather than a story "written." We may now consider the significance of the next phrase of that definition, which states that a play is devised to be "presented," rather than to be "read."

The only way in which it is possible to study most of the great plays of bygone ages is to read the record of their dialogue; and this necessity has led to the academic fallacy of considering great plays primarily as compositions to be read. In their own age, however, these very plays which we now read in the closet were intended primarily to be presented on the stage. Really to read a play requires a very special and difficult exercise of visual imagination. It is necessary not only to appreciate the dialogue, but also to project before the mind's eye a vivid imagined rendition of the visual aspect of the action. This is the reason why most managers and stage-directors are unable to judge conclusively the merits and defects of a new play from reading it in manuscript. One of our most subtle artists in stage-direction, **Mr. Henry Miller**, once confessed to the present writer that he could never decide whether a prospective play was good or bad until he had seen it re-hearsed by actors on a stage. Mr. Augustus Thomas's unusually successful farce entitled *Mrs. Leffingwell's Boots* was considered a failure by its producing managers until the very last rehearsals, because it depended for its finished effect on many intricate and rapid intermovements of the actors, which until the last moment were understood and realised only in the mind of the playwright. The same author's best and most successful play, *The Witching Hour*, was declined by several managers before it was ultimately accepted for production; and the reason was, presumably, that its extraordinary merits were not manifest from a mere reading of the lines. If professional producers may go so far astray in their judgment of the merits of a manuscript, how much harder must it be for the layman to judge a play solely from a reading of the dialogue!

This fact should lead the professors and the students in our colleges to adopt a very tentative attitude toward judging the dramatic merits of the plays of other ages. Shakespeare, considered as a poet, is so immeasurably superior to Dryden, that it is difficult for the college student unfamiliar with the theatre to realise that the former's *Antony and Cleopatra* is, considered solely as a play, far inferior to the latter's dramatisation of the same story, entitled *All for Love, or The World Well Lost*. Shakespeare's play upon this subject follows closely the chronology of Plutarch's narrative, and is merely dramatised history; but Dryden's play is reconstructed with a more practical sense of economy and emphasis, and deserves to be regarded as historical drama. *Cymbeline* is, in many passages, so greatly written that it is hard for the closet-student to realise that it is a bad play, even when considered from the standpoint of the Elizabethan theatre,— whereas *Othello* and *Macbeth*, for instance, are great plays, not only of their age but for all time. *King Lear* is probably a more sublime poem than *Othello;* and it is only by seeing the two pieces performed equally well in the theatre that we can appreciate by what a wide margin *Othello* is the better play.

This practical point has been felt emphatically by the very greatest dramatists; and this fact offers, of course, an explanation of the otherwise inexplicable negligence of such authors as Shakespeare and Molière in the matter of publishing their plays. These supreme playwrights wanted people to see their pieces in the theatre rather than to read them in the closet. In his own lifetime, Shakespeare, who was very scrupulous about the publication of his sonnets and his narrative poems, printed a carefully edited text of his plays only when he was forced, in self-defense, to do so, by the prior appearance of corrupt and pirated editions; and we owe our present knowledge of several of his dramas merely to the business acumen of two actors who, seven years after his death, conceived the practical idea that they might turn an easy penny by printing and offering for sale the text of several popular plays which the public had already seen performed. Sardou, who, like most French dramatists, began by publishing his plays, carefully withheld from print the master-efforts of his prime; and even such dramatists as habitually print their plays prefer nearly always to have them seen first and read only afterwards.

In elucidation of what might otherwise seem perversity on the part of great dramatic authors like Shakespeare, we must remember that the master-dramatists have nearly always been men of the theatre rather than men of letters, and therefore naturally more avid of immediate success with a contemporary audience than of posthumous success with a posterity of readers. Shakespeare and Molière were actors and theatre-managers, and devised their plays primarily for the patrons of the Globe and the Palais Royal. Ibsen, who is often taken as a type of the literary dramatist, derived his early training mainly from the profession of the theatre and hardly at all from the profession of letters. For half a dozen years, during the formative period of his twenties, he acted as producing manager of the National Theatre in Bergen, and learned the tricks of his trade from studying the masterpieces of contemporary drama, mainly of the French school. In his own work, he began, in such pieces as *Lady Inger of Ostrat*, by imitating and applying the formulas of Scribe and the earlier Sardou; and it was only after many years that he marched forward to a technique entirely his own. Both Sir Arthur Wing Pinero and Mr. Stephen Phillips began their theatrical career as actors. On the other hand, men of letters who have written works primarily to be read have almost never succeeded as dramatists. In England, during the nineteenth century, the following great poets all tried their hands at plays — Scott, Southey, Wordsworth, Coleridge, Byron, Shelley, Keats, Browning, Mrs. Browning, Matthew Arnold, Swinburne, and Tennyson — and not one of them produced a work of any considerable value from the standpoint of dramatic criticism. Tennyson, in *Becket*, came nearer to the mark than any of the others; and it is noteworthy that, in this work, he had the advantage of the advice and, in a sense, collaboration of Sir Henry Irving.

The familiar phrase " closet-drama " is a contradiction of terms. The species of literary composition in dialogue that is ordinarily so desig-

nated occupies a thoroughly legitimate position in
the realm of literature, but no position whatsoever
in the realm of dramaturgy.   *Atalanta in Calydon*
is a great poem; but from the standpoint of the
theory of the theatre, it cannot be considered as
a play.   Like the lyric poems of the same author,
it was written to be read; and it was not devised
to be presented by actors on a stage before an
audience.

We may now consider the significance of the
three concluding phrases of the definition of a
play which was offered at the outset of the present chapter.   These phrases indicate the immanence
of three influences by which the work of the playwright is constantly conditioned.

In the first place, by the fact that the dramatist
is devising his story for the use of actors, he is
definitely limited both in respect to the kind of
characters he may create and in respect to the
means he may employ in order to delineate them.
In actual life we meet characters of two different
classes, which (borrowing a pair of adjectives from
the terminology of physics) we may denominate
dynamic characters and static characters.   But
when an actor appears upon the stage, he wants to
act; and the dramatist is therefore obliged to confine his attention to dynamic characters, and to exclude static characters almost entirely from the
range of his creation.   The essential trait of all

dynamic characters is the preponderance within them of the element of will; and the persons of a play must therefore be people with active wills and emphatic intentions. When such people are brought into juxtaposition, there necessarily results a clash of contending desires and purposes; and by this fact we are led logically to the conclusion that the proper subject-matter of the drama is a struggle between contrasted human wills. The same conclusion, as we shall notice in the next chapter, may be reached logically by deduction from the natural demands of an assembled audience; and the subject will be discussed more fully during the course of our study of *The Psychology of Theatre Audiences*. At present it is sufficient for us to note that every great play that has ever been devised has presented some phase or other of this single, necessary theme,— a contention of individual human wills. An actor, moreover, is always more effective in scenes of emotion than in scenes of cold logic and calm reason; and the dramatist, therefore, is obliged to select as his leading figures people whose acts are motivated by emotion rather than by intellect. Aristotle, for example, would make a totally uninteresting figure if he were presented faithfully upon the stage. Who could imagine Darwin as the hero of a drama? Othello, on the other hand, is not at all a reasonable being; from first to last his intellect is " perplexed in the extreme." His emotions are the motives for his acts; and in this he may be taken as the type of a dramatic character.

In the means of delineating the characters he has imagined, the dramatist, because he is writing for actors, is more narrowly restricted than the novelist. His people must constantly be doing something, and must therefore reveal themselves mainly through their acts. They may, of course, also be delineated through their way of saying things; but in the theatre the objective action is always more suggestive than the spoken word. We know Sherlock Holmes, in Mr. William Gillette's admirable melodrama, solely through the things that we have seen him do; and in this connection we should remember that in the stories by Sir Arthur Conan Doyle from which Mr. Gillette derived his narrative material, Holmes is delineated largely by a very different method,— the method, namely, of expository comment written from the point of view of Doctor Watson. A leading actor seldom wants to sit in his dressing-room while he is being talked about by the other actors on the stage; and therefore the method of drawing character by comment, which is so useful for the novelist, is rarely employed by the playwright except in the waste moments which precede the first entrance of his leading figure. The Chorus Lady, in Mr. James Forbes's amusing study of that name, is drawn chiefly through her way of saying things; but though this method of delineation is sometimes very effective for an act or two, it can seldom be sustained without a faltering of interest through a full-grown four-act play. The novelist's expedient of delineating character through mental analysis is of course denied the dramatist, especially in this modern age when the soliloquy (for reasons which will be noted in a subsequent chapter) is usually frowned upon. Sometimes, in the theatre, a character may be exhibited chiefly through his personal effect upon the other people on the stage, and thereby indirectly on the people in the audience. It was in this way, of course, that Manson was delineated in Mr. Charles Rann Kennedy's *The Servant in the House*. But the expedient is a dangerous one for the dramatist to use; because it makes his work immediately dependent on the actor chosen for the leading role, and may in many cases render his play impossible of attaining its full effect except at the hands of a single great performer. In recent years an expedient long familiar in the novel has been transferred to the service of the stage,— the expedient, namely, of suggesting the personality of a character through a visual presentation of his habitual environment. After the curtain had been raised upon the first act of *The Music Master*, and the audience had been given time to look about the room which was represented on the stage, the main traits of the leading character had already been suggested before his first appearance on the scene. The pictures and knickknacks on his mantelpiece told us, before we ever saw him, what manner of man he was. But such subtle means as this can, after all, be used only to reinforce the one standard method of conveying the sense of character in drama; and this one method, owing to the conditions under which the playwright does his work, must always be the exhibition of objective acts.

In all these general ways the work of the dramatist is affected by the fact that he must devise his story to be presented by actors. The specific influence exerted over the playwright by the individual performer is a subject too extensive to be covered by a mere summary consideration in the present context; and we shall therefore discuss it fully in a later chapter, entitled *The Actor and the Dramatist*.

At present we must pass on to observe that, in the second place, the work of the dramatist is conditioned by the fact that he must plan his plays to fit the sort of theatre that stands ready to receive them. A fundamental and necessary relation has always existed between theatre-building and theatric art. The best plays of any period have been fashioned in accordance with the physical conditions of the best theatres of that period.

Therefore, in order fully to appreciate such a play as *Œdipus King*, it is necessary to imagine the theatre of Dionysus; and in order to understand thoroughly the dramaturgy of Shakespeare and Molière, it is necessary to reconstruct in retrospect the altered inn-yard and the converted tennis-court for which they planned their plays. It may seriously be doubted that the works of these earlier masters gain more than they lose from being produced with the elaborate scenic accessories of the modern stage; and, on the other hand, a modern play by Ibsen or Pinero would lose three-fourths of its effect if it were acted in the Elizabethan manner, or produced without scenery (let us say) in the Roman theatre at Orange.

Since, in all ages, the size and shape and physical appointments of the theatre have determined for the playwright the form and structure of his plays, we may always explain the stock conventions of any period of the drama by referring to the physical aspect of the theatre in that period. Let us consider briefly, for purposes of illustration, certain obvious ways in which the art of the great Greek tragic dramatists was affected by the nature of the Attic stage. The theatre of Dionysus was an enormous edifice carved out of a hillside. It was so large that the dramatists were obliged to deal only with subjects that were traditional,— stories which had long been familiar to the entire theatre-going public, including the poorer and less educated spectators who sat farthest from the actors. Since most of the audience was grouped above the stage and at a considerable distance, the actors, in order not to appear dwarfed, were obliged to walk on stilted boots. A performer so accoutred could not move impetuously or enact a scene of violence; and this practical limitation is sufficient to account for the measured and majestic movement of Greek tragedy, and the convention that murders and other violent deeds must always be imagined off the stage and be merely recounted to the audience by messengers. Facial expression could not be seen in so large a theatre; and the actors therefore wore masks, conventionalised to represent the dominant mood of a character during a scene. This limitation forced the performer to depend for his effect mainly on his voice; and Greek tragedy was therefore necessarily more lyrical than later types of drama.

The few points which we have briefly touched upon are usually explained, by academic critics, on literary grounds; but it is surely more sane to explain them on grounds of common sense, in the light of what we know of the conditions of the Attic stage. Similarly, it would be easy to show how Terence and Calderon, Shakespeare and Molière, adapted the form of their plays to the form of their theatres; but enough has already been said to indicate the principle which underlies this particular phase of the theory of the theatre. The successive changes in the physical aspect of the English theatre during the last three centuries have all tended toward greater naturalness, intimacy, and subtlety, in the drama itself and in the physical aids to its presentment. This progress, with its constant illustration of the interdependence of the drama and the stage, may most conveniently be studied in historical review; and to such a review we shall devote a special chapter, entitled *Stage Conventions in Modern Times.*

We may now observe that, in the third place, the essential nature of the drama is affected greatly by the fact that it is destined to be set before an audience. The dramatist must appeal at once to a heterogeneous multitude of people; and the full effect of this condition will be investigated in a special chapter on *The Psychology of Theatre Audiences.* In an important sense, the audience is a party to the play, and collaborates with the actors in the presentation. This fact, which remains often unappreciated by academic critics, is familiar to everyone who has had any practical association with the theatre. It is almost never possible, even for trained dramatic critics, to tell from a final dress-rehearsal in an empty house which scenes of a new play are fully effective and which are not; and the reason why, in America, new plays

are tried out on the road is not so much to give
the actors practice in their parts, as to determine,
from the effect of the piece upon provincial audiences, whether it is worthy of a metropolitan
presentation.   The point is, as we shall notice in
the next chapter, that since a play is devised
for a crowd it cannot finally be judged by individuals.

The dependence of the dramatist upon his audience may be illustrated by the history of many important plays, which, though effective in their own
age, have become ineffective for later generations,
solely because they were founded on certain general
principles of conduct in which the world has sub-
sequently ceased to believe.   From the point of
view of its own period, *The Maid's Tragedy* of
Beaumont and Fletcher is undoubtedly one of the
very greatest of Elizabethan plays; but it would
be ineffective in the modern theatre, because it presupposes a principle which a contemporary audience would not accept.   It was devised for an
audience of aristocrats in the reign of James I,
and the dramatic struggle is founded upon the
doctrine of the divine right of kings.   Amintor,
in the play, has suffered a profound personal injury at the hands of his sovereign; but he cannot
avenge this individual disgrace, because he is a subject of the royal malefactor.   The crisis and turn-
ing-point of the entire drama is a scene in which

Amintor, with the king at his mercy, lowers his
sword with the words:—

> But there is
> Divinity about you, that strikes dead
> My rising passions: as you are my king,
> I fall before you, and present my sword
> To cut mine own flesh, if it be your will.

We may imagine the applause of the courtiers of
James Stuart, the Presumptuous; but never since
the Cromwellian revolution has that scene been
really effective on the English stage. In order
fully to appreciate a dramatic struggle, an audience must sympathise with the motives that occasion it.

It should now be evident, as was suggested at
the outset, that all the leading principles of the
theory of the theatre may be deduced logically
from the axiom which was stated in the first sentence of this chapter; and that axiom should constantly be borne in mind as the basis of all our
subsequent discussions. But in view of several important points which have already come up for
consideration, it may be profitable, before relin-
quishing our initial question, to redefine a play
more fully in the following terms:—

A play is a representation, by actors, on a stage,
before an audience, of a struggle between individual human wills, motivated by emotion rather than
by intellect, and expressed in terms of objective
action.

II

THE PSYCHOLOGY OF THEATRE AUDI-
ENCES

I

THE drama is the only art, excepting oratory
and certain forms of music, that is designed to
appeal to a crowd instead of to an individual.
The lyric poet writes for himself, and for such
selected persons here and there throughout the
world as may be wisely sympathetic enough to understand his musings. The essayist and the novelist
write for a reader sitting alone in his library:
whether ten such readers or a hundred thousand
ultimately read a book, the writer speaks to each
of them apart from all the others. It is the same
with painting and with sculpture. Though a picture or a statue may be seen by a limitless succession
of observers, its appeal is made always to the individual mind. But it is different with a play. Since a
drama is, in essence, a story devised to be presented
by actors on a stage before an audience, it must
necessarily be designed to appeal at once to a multitude of people. We have to be alone in order to
appreciate the *Venus of Melos* or the *Sistine Ma-*

donna or the *Ode to a Nightingale* or the *Egoist* or the *Religio Medici;* but who could sit alone in a wide theatre and see *Cyrano de Bergerac* performed? The sympathetic presence of a multitude of people would be as necessary to our appreciation of the play as solitude in all the other cases. And because the drama must be written for a crowd, it must be fashioned differently from the other, and less popular, forms of art.

No writer is really a dramatist unless he recognises this distinction of appeal; and if an author is not accustomed to writing for the crowd, he can hardly hope to make a satisfying play. Tennyson, the perfect poet; Browning, the master of the human mind; Stevenson, the teller of enchanting tales: — each of them failed when he tried to make a drama, because the conditions of his proper art had schooled him long in writing for the individual instead of for the crowd. A literary artist who writes for the individual may produce a great work of literature that is cast in the dramatic form; but the work will not be, in the practical sense, a play. *Samson Agonistes, Faust, Pippa Passes, Peer Gynt,* and the early dream-dramas of Maurice Maeterlinck, are something else than plays. They are not devised to be presented by actors on a stage before an audience. As a work of literature, *A Blot in the 'Scutcheon* is immeasurably greater than *The Two Orphans;* but as a play, it is immeasurably less. For even though, in this particular piece, Browning did try to write for the theatre (at the suggestion of Macready), he employed the same intricately intellectual method of character analysis that has made many of his poems the most solitude-compelling of modern literary works. Properly to appreciate his piece, you must be alone, just as you must be alone to read *A Woman's Last Word*. It is not written for a crowd; *The Two Orphans*, less weighty in wisdom, is. The second is a play.

The mightiest masters of the drama — Sophocles, Shakespeare, and Molière — have recognised the popular character of its appeal and written frankly for the multitude. The crowd, therefore, has exercised a potent influence upon the dramatist in every era of the theatre. One person the lyric poet has to please,— himself; to a single person only, or an unlimited succession of single persons, does the novelist address himself, and he may choose the sort of person he will write for; but the dramatist must always please the many. His themes, his thoughts, his emotions, are circumscribed by the limits of popular appreciation. He writes less freely than any other author; for he cannot pick his auditors. Mr. Henry James may, if he choose, write novels for the super-civilised; but a crowd is never super-civilised, and therefore characters like those of Mr. James could never be successfully presented in the theatre. *Treasure Island* is a book for boys, both young and old; but a modern theatre crowd is composed largely of women, and the theme of such a story could scarcely be successful on the stage.

In order, therefore, to understand the limitations of the drama as an art, and clearly to define its scope, it is necessary to inquire into the psychology of theatre audiences. This subject presents two phases to the student. First, a theatre audience exhibits certain psychological traits that are common to all crowds, of whatever kind,— a political convention, the spectators at a ball-game, or a church congregation, for example. Second, it exhibits certain other traits which distinguish it from other kinds of crowds. These, in turn, will be considered in the present chapter.

II

By the word *crowd*, as it is used in this discussion, is meant a multitude of people whose ideas and feelings have taken a set in a certain single direction, and who, because of this, exhibit a tendency to lose their individual self-consciousness in the general self-consciousness of the multitude. Any gathering of people for a specific purpose — whether of action or of worship or of amusement — tends to become, because of this purpose, a *crowd*, in the scientific sense. Now, a crowd has a mind of its own, apart from that of any of its individual members. The psychology of the crowd was little understood until late in the nineteenth century, when a great deal of attention was turned to it by a group of French philosophers. The subject has been most fully studied by M. Gustave Le Bon, who devoted some two hundred pages to his *Psychologie des Foules*. According to M. Le Bon, a man, by the mere fact that he forms a factor of a crowd, tends to lose consciousness of those mental qualities in which he differs from his fellows, and becomes more keenly conscious than before of those other mental qualities in which he is at one with them. The mental qualities in which men differ from one another are the acquired qualities of intellect and character; but the qualities in which they are at one are the innate basic passions of the race. A crowd, therefore, is less intellectual and more emotional than the individuals that compose it. It is less reasonable, less judicious, less disinterested, more credulous, more primitive, more partisan; and hence, as M. Le Bon cleverly puts it, a man, by the mere fact that he forms a part of an organised crowd, is likely to descend several rungs on the ladder of civilisation. Even the most cultured and intellectual of men, when he forms an atom of a crowd, tends to lose consciousness of his acquired mental qualities and to revert to his primal simplicity and sensitiveness of mind.

The dramatist, therefore, because he writes for a crowd, writes for a comparatively uncivilised and uncultivated mind, a mind richly human, vehement in approbation, emphatic in disapproval, easily credulous, eagerly enthusiastic, boyishly heroic, and somewhat carelessly unthinking. Now, it has been found in practice that the only thing that will keenly interest a crowd is a struggle of some sort or other. Speaking empirically, the late Ferdinand Brunetière, in 1893, stated that the drama has dealt always with a struggle between human wills; and his statement, formulated in the catch-phrase, " No struggle, no drama," has since become a commonplace of dramatic criticism. But, so far as I know, no one has yet realised the main reason for this, which is, simply, that characters are interesting to a crowd only in those crises of emotion that bring them to the grapple. A single individual, like the reader of an essay or a novel, may be interested intellectually in those gentle influences beneath which a character unfolds itself as mildly as a water-lily; but to what Thackeray called " that savage child, the crowd," a character does not appeal except in moments of contention. There never yet has been a time when the theatre could compete successfully against the amphitheatre. Plautus and Terence complained that the Roman public preferred a gladiatorial combat to their plays; a bear-baiting or a cock-fight used to empty

Shakespeare's theatre on the Bankside; and there is not a matinée in town to-day that can hold its own against a foot-ball game. Forty thousand people gather annually from all quarters of the East to see Yale and Harvard meet upon the field, while such a crowd could not be aggregated from New York alone to see the greatest play the world has yet produced. For the crowd demands a fight; and where the actual exists, it will scarcely be contented with the semblance.

Hence the drama, to interest at all, must cater to this longing for contention, which is one of the primordial instincts of the crowd. It must present its characters in some struggle of the wills, whether it be flippant, as in the case of Benedick and Beatrice; or delicate, as in that of Viola and Orsino; or terrible, with Macbeth; or piteous, with Lear. The crowd is more partisan than the individual; and therefore, in following this struggle of the drama, it desires always to take sides. There is no fun in seeing a foot-ball game unless you care about who wins; and there is very little fun in seeing a play unless the dramatist allows you to throw your sympathies on one side or the other of the struggle. Hence, although in actual life both parties to a conflict are often partly right and partly wrong, and it is hard to choose between them, the dramatist usually simplifies the struggle in his plays by throwing the balance of right

strongly on one side. Hence, from the ethical
standpoint, the simplicity of theatre characters.
Desdemona is all innocence, Iago all deviltry.
Hence also the conventional heroes and villains of
melodrama,— these to be hissed and those to be
applauded. Since the crowd is comparatively lacking in the judicial faculty and cannot look upon
a play from a detached and disinterested point of
view, it is either all for or all against a character;
and in either case its judgment is frequently in
defiance of the rules of reason. It will hear no
word against Camille, though an individual would
judge her to be wrong, and it has no sympathy
with Père Duval. It idolizes Raffles, who is a liar
and a thief; it shuts its ears to Marion Allardyce,
the defender of virtue in *Letty*. It wants its sympathetic characters, to love; its antipathetic characters, to hate; and it hates and loves them as un-
reasonably as a savage or a child. The trouble
with *Hedda Gabler* as a play is that it contains not
a single personage that the audience can love.
The crowd demands those so-called " sympathetic "
parts that every actor, for this reason, longs to
represent. And since the crowd is partisan, it
wants its favored characters to win. Hence the
convention of the " happy ending," insisted on by
managers who feel the pulse of the public. The
blind Louise, in *The Two Orphans*, will get her
sight back, never fear. Even the wicked Oliver,

in *As You Like It*, must turn over a new leaf and marry a pretty girl.

Next to this prime instinct of partisanship in watching a contention, one of the most important traits in the psychology of crowds is their extreme credulity. A crowd will nearly always believe anything that it sees and almost anything that it is told. An audience composed entirely of individuals who have no belief in ghosts will yet accept the Ghost in *Hamlet* as a fact. Bless you, they have *seen* him! The crowd accepts the disguise of Rosalind, and never wonders why Orlando does not recognise his love. To this extreme credulity of the crowd is due the long line of plays that are founded on mistaken identity,— farces like *The Comedy of Errors* and melodramas like *The Lyons Mail*, for example. The crowd, too, will accept without demur any condition precedent to the story of a play, however impossible it might seem to the mind of the individual. Œdipus King has been married to his mother many years before the play begins; but the Greek crowd forbore to ask why, in so long a period, the enormity had never been discovered. The central situation of *She Stoops to Conquer* seems impossible to the individual mind, but is eagerly accepted by the crowd. Individual critics find fault with Thomas Heywood's lovely old play, *A Woman Killed with Kindness*, on the ground that though Frankford's noble forgiveness of his erring wife is beautiful to contemplate, Mrs. Frankford's infidelity is not sufficiently motivated, and the whole story, therefore, is untrue. But Heywood, writing for the crowd, said frankly, " If you will grant that Mrs. Frankford was unfaithful, I can tell you a lovely story about her husband, who was a gentleman worth knowing: otherwise there can't be any story "; and the Elizabethan crowd, eager for the story, was willing to oblige the dramatist with the necessary credulity.

There is this to be said about the credulity of an audience, however,— that it will believe what it sees much more readily than what it hears. It might not believe in the ghost of Hamlet's father if the ghost were merely spoken of and did not walk upon the stage. If a dramatist would convince his audience of the generosity or the treachery of one character or another, he should not waste words either praising or blaming the character, but should present him to the eye in the performance of a generous or treacherous action. The audience *hears* wise words from Polonius when he gives his parting admonition to his son; but the same audience *sees* him made a fool of by Prince Hamlet, and will not think him wise.

The fact that a crowd's eyes are more keenly receptive than its ears is the psychologic basis for the maxim that in the theatre action speaks louder than words. It also affords a reason why plays of which the audience does not understand a single word are frequently successful. Mme. Sarah Bernhardt's thrilling performance of *La Tosca* has always aroused enthusiasm in London and New York, where the crowd, as a crowd, could not understand the language of the play.

Another primal characteristic of the mind of the crowd is its susceptibility to emotional contagion. A cultivated individual reading *The School for Scandal* at home alone will be intelligently appreciative of its delicious humor; but it is difficult to imagine him laughing over it aloud. Yet the same individual, when submerged in a theatre crowd, will laugh heartily over this very play, largely because other people near him are laughing too. Laughter, tears, enthusiasm, all the basic human emotions, thrill and tremble through an audience, because each member of the crowd feels that he is surrounded by other people who are experiencing the same emotion as his own. In the sad part of a play it is hard to keep from weeping if the woman next to you is wiping her eyes; and still harder is it to keep from laughing, even at a sorry jest, if the man on the other side is roaring in vociferous cachinnation. Successful dramatists play upon the susceptibility of a crowd by serving up raw morsels of crude humor and pathos for the unthinking to wheeze and blubber over, knowing that these members of the audience will excite their more phlegmatic neighbors by contagion. The practical dictum that every laugh in the first act is worth money in the box-office is founded on this psychologic truth.   Even puns as bad as Mr. Zangwill's are of value early in a play to set on some quantity of barren spectators and get the house accustomed to a titter.   Scenes like the football episodes in *The College Widow* and *Strongheart*, or the battle in *The Round Up*, are nearly always sure to raise the roof; for it is usually sufficient to set everybody on the stage a-cheering in order to make the audience cheer too by sheer contagion.   Another and more classical example was the speechless triumph of Henry V's return victorious, in Richard Mansfield's sumptuous production of the play.   Here the audience felt that he was every inch a king; for it had caught the fervor of the crowd upon the stage.

This same emotional contagion is, of course, the psychologic basis for the French system of the *claque*, or band of hired applauders seated in the centre of the house.   The leader of the *claque* knows his cues as if he were an actor in the piece, and at the psychologic moment the *claqueurs* burst forth with their clatter and start the house applauding.   Applause begets applause in the theatre, as laughter begets laughter and tears beget tears.

But not only is the crowd more emotional than

the individual; it is also more sensuous. It has the lust of the eye and of the ear,— the savage's love of gaudy color, the child's love of soothing sound. It is fond of flaring flags and blaring trumpets. Hence the rich-costumed processions of the Elizabethan stage, many years before the use of scenery; and hence, in our own day, the success of pieces like *The Darling of the Gods* and *The Rose of the Rancho*. Color, light, and music, artistically blended, will hold the crowd better than the most absorbing story. This is the reason for the vogue of musical comedy, with its pretty girls, and gaudy shifts of scenery and lights, and tricksy, tripping melodies and dances.

Both in its sentiments and in its opinions, the crowd is comfortably commonplace. It is, as a crowd, incapable of original thought and of any but inherited emotion. It has no speculation in its eyes. What it feels was felt before the flood; and what it thinks, its fathers thought before it. The most effective moments in the theatre are those that appeal to basic and commonplace emotions, — love of woman, love of home, love of country, love of right, anger, jealousy, revenge, ambition, lust, and treachery. So great for centuries has been the inherited influence of the Christian religion that any adequate play whose motive is self-sacrifice is almost certain to succeed. Even when the self-sacrifice is unwise and ignoble, as in the first act of *Frou-Frou*, the crowd will give it vehement approval. Countless plays have been made upon the man who unselfishly assumes responsibility for another's guilt. The great tragedies have familiar themes,— ambition in *Macbeth*, jealousy in *Othello*, filial ingratitude in *Lear;* there is nothing in these motives that the most unthinking audience could fail to understand. No crowd can resist the fervor of a patriot who goes down scornful before many spears. Show the audience a flag to die for, or a stalking ghost to be avenged, or a shred of honor to maintain against agonizing odds, and it will thrill with an enthusiasm as ancient as the human race. Few are the plays that can succeed without the moving force of love, the most familiar of all emotions. These themes do not require that the audience shall think.

But for the speculative, the original, the new, the crowd evinces little favor. If the dramatist holds ideas of religion, or of politics, or of social law, that are in advance of his time, he must keep them to himself or else his plays will fail. Nimble wits, like Mr. Shaw, who scorn tradition, can attain a popular success only through the crowd's inherent love of fads; they cannot long succeed when they run counter to inherited ideas. The great successful dramatists, like Molière and Shakespeare, have always thought with the crowd on all essential questions. Their views of religion, of morality, of politics, of law, have been the views of the populace, nothing more. They never raise questions that cannot quickly be answered by the crowd, through the instinct of inherited experience. No mind was ever, in the philosophic sense, more commonplace than that of Shakespeare. He had no new ideas. He was never radical, and seldom even progressive. He was a careful money-making business man, fond of food and drink and out-of-doors and laughter, a patriot, a lover, and a gentleman. Greatly did he know things about people; greatly, also, could he write. But he accepted the religion, the politics, and the social ethics of his time, without ever bothering to wonder if these things might be improved.

The great speculative spirits of the world, those who overturn tradition and discover new ideas, have had minds far different from this. They have not written plays. It is to these men,— the philosopher, the essayist, the novelist, the lyric poet,— that each of us turns for what is new in thought. But from the dramatist the crowd desires only the old, old thought. It has no patience for consideration; it will listen only to what it knows already. If, therefore, a great man has a new doctrine to expound, let him set it forth in a book of essays; or, if he needs must sugar-coat it with a story, let him expound it in a novel, whose appeal will be to the individual mind. Not until a doctrine is old

enough to have become generally accepted is it
ripe for exploitation in the theatre.

This point is admirably illustrated by two of
the best and most successful plays of recent seasons.
The Witching Hour, by Mr. Augustus Thomas,
and *The Servant in the House*, by Mr. Charles
Rann Kennedy, were both praised by many critics
for their " novelty "; but to me one of the most
significant and instructive facts about them is that
neither of them was, in any real respect, novel in
the least.   Consider for a moment the deliberate
and careful lack of novelty in the ideas which Mr.
Thomas so skilfully set forth.   What Mr. Thomas
really did was to gather and arrange as many as
possible of the popularly current thoughts concerning telepathy and cognate subjects, and to tell
the public what they themselves had been wondering about and thinking during the last few years.
The timeliness of the play lay in the fact that it
was produced late enough in the history of its
subject to be selectively resumptive, and not nearly
so much in the fact that it was produced early
enough to forestall other dramatic presentations of
the same materials.   Mr. Thomas has himself explained, in certain semi-public conversations, that
he postponed the composition of this play — on
which his mind had been set for many years —
until the general public had become sufficiently accustomed to the ideas which he intended to set

forth. Ten years before, this play would have
been novel, and would undoubtedly have failed.
When it was produced, it was not novel, but resumptive, in its thought; and therefore it succeeded. For one of the surest ways of succeeding
in the theatre is to sum up and present dramatically
all that the crowd has been thinking for some time
concerning any subject of importance. The dramatist should be the catholic collector and wise in-
terpreter of those ideas which the crowd, in its
conservatism, feels already to be safely true.

And if *The Servant in the House* will — as I
believe — outlive *The Witching Hour,* it will be
mainly because, in the author's theme and his
ideas, it is older by many, many centuries. The
theme of Mr. Thomas's play — namely, that
thought is in itself a dynamic force and has the
virtue and to some extent the power of action —
is, as I have just explained, not novel, but is at
least recent in the history of thinking. It is a
theme which dates itself as belonging to the present generation, and is likely to lose interest for
the next. But Mr. Kennedy's theme — namely,
that when discordant human beings ascend to meet
each other in the spirit of brotherly love, it may
truly be said that God is resident among them —
is at least as old as the gentle-hearted Galilean,
and, being dateless, belongs to future generations
as well as to the present. Mr. Thomas has been

skilfully resumptive of a passing period of popular thought; but Mr. Kennedy has been resumptive on a larger scale, and has built his play upon the wisdom of the centuries.   Paradoxical as it may seem, the very reason why *The Servant in the House* struck so many critics as being strange and new is that, in its thesis and its thought, it is as old as the world.

The truth of this point seems to me indisputable. I know that the best European playwrights of the present day are striving to use the drama as a vehicle for the expression of advanced ideas, especially in regard to social ethics; but in doing this, I think, they are mistaking the scope of the theatre. They are striving to say in the drama what might be said better in the essay or the novel.   As the exposition of a theory, Mr. Shaw's *Man and Superman* is not nearly so effective as the writings of Schopenhauer and Nietzsche, from whom the playwright borrowed his ideas.   The greatest works of Ibsen can be appreciated only by the cultured individual and not by the uncultured crowd.   That is why the breadth of his appeal will never equal that of Shakespeare, in spite of his unfathomable intellect and his perfect mastery of the technique of his art.   Only his more commonplace plays — *A Doll's House*, for example — have attained a wide success.   And a wide success is a thing to be desired for other than material reasons.   Surely it is a good thing for the public that *Hamlet* never fails.

The conservatism of the greatest dramatists asserts itself not only in their thoughts but even in the mere form of their plays.   It is the lesser men who invent new tricks of technique and startle the public with innovations.   Molière merely perfected the type of Italian comedy that his public long had known.   Shakespeare quietly adopted the forms that lesser men had made the crowd familiar with.   He imitated Lyly in *Love's Labour's Lost*, Greene in *As You Like It*, Marlowe in *Richard III*, Kyd in *Hamlet*, and Fletcher in *The Tempest*. He did the old thing better than the other men had done it,— that is all.

Yet this is greatly to Shakespeare's credit.   He was wise enough to feel that what the crowd wanted, both in matter and in form, was what was needed in the greatest drama.   In saying that Shakespeare's mind was commonplace, I meant to tender him the highest praise.   In his commonplaceness lies his sanity.   He is so greatly *usual* that he can understand all men and sympathise with them.   He is above novelty.   His wisdom is greater than the wisdom of the few; he is the heir of all the ages, and draws his wisdom from the general mind of man.   And it is largely because of this that he represents ever the ideal of the dramatist.   He who would write for the theatre must not despise the crowd.

III

All of the above-mentioned characteristics of theatre audiences, their instinct for contention and for partisanship, their credulity, their sensuousness, their susceptibility to emotional contagion, their incapacity for original thought, their conservatism, and their love of the commonplace, appear in every sort of crowd, as M. Le Bon has proved with ample illustration.   It remains for us to notice certain traits in which theatre audiences differ from other kinds of crowds.

In the first place, a theatre audience is composed of individuals more heterogeneous than those that make up a political, or social, or sporting, or religious convocation.   The crowd at a foot-ball game, at a church, at a social or political convention, is by its very purpose selective of its elements : it is made up entirely of college-folk, or Presbyterians, or Prohibitionists, or Republicans, as the case may be.   But a theatre audience is composed of all sorts and conditions of men.   The same theatre in New York contains the rich and the poor, the literate and the illiterate, the old and the young, the native and the naturalised.   The same play, therefore, must appeal to all of these.   It follows that the dramatist must be broader in his

appeal than any other artist. He cannot confine
his message to any single caste of society. In the
same single work of art he must incorporate elements that will interest all classes of humankind.

Those promising dramatic movements that have
confined their appeal to a certain single stratum of
society have failed ever, because of this, to achieve
the highest excellence. The trouble with Roman
comedy is that it was written for an audience composed chiefly of freedmen and slaves. The patrician caste of Rome walked wide of the theatres.
Only the dregs of society gathered to applaud the
comedies of Plautus and Terence. Hence the over-
simplicity of their prologues, and their tedious repetition of the obvious. Hence, also, their vul-
garity, their horse-play, their obscenity. Here was
fine dramatic genius led astray, because the time
was out of joint. Similarly, the trouble with
French tragedy, in the classicist period of Corneille
and Racine, is that it was written only for the
finest caste of society,— the patrician coterie of a
patrician cardinal. Hence its over-niceness, and
its appeal to the ear rather than to the eye. Terence aimed too low and Racine aimed too high.
Each of them, therefore, shot wide of the mark;
while Molière, who wrote at once for patrician and
plebeian, scored a hit.

The really great dramatic movements of the
world — that of Spain in the age of Calderon and

Lope, that of England in the spacious times of great Elizabeth, that of France from 1830 to the present hour — have broadened their appeal to every class. The queen and the orange-girl joyed together in the healthiness of Rosalind; the king and the gamin laughed together at the rogueries of Scapin. The breadth of Shakespeare's appeal remains one of the most significant facts in the history of the drama. Tell a filthy-faced urchin of the gutter that you know about a play that shows a ghost that stalks and talks at midnight underneath a castle-tower, and a man that makes believe he is out of his head so that he can get the better of a wicked king, and a girl that goes mad and drowns herself, and a play within the play, and a funeral in a churchyard, and a duel with poisoned swords, and a great scene at the end in which nearly every one gets killed: tell him this, and watch his eyes grow wide! I have been to a thirty-cent performance of *Othello* in a middle-western town, and have felt the audience thrill with the headlong hurry of the action. Yet these are the plays that cloistered students study for their wisdom and their style!

And let us not forget, in this connection, that a similar breadth of appeal is neither necessary nor greatly to be desired in those forms of literature that, unlike the drama, are not written for the crowd. The greatest non-dramatic poet and the

greatest novelist in English are appreciated only
by the few; but this is not in the least to the dis-
credit of Milton and of Meredith.   One indication
of the greatness of Mr. Kipling's story, *They*, is
that very few have learned to read it.

Victor Hugo, in his preface to *Ruy Blas*, has
discussed this entire principle from a slightly different point of view.   He divides the theatre audience into three classes — the thinkers, who
demand characterisation; the women, who demand
passion; and the mob, who demand action — and
insists that every great play must appeal to all
three classes at once.   Certainly *Ruy Blas* itself
fulfils this desideratum, and is great in the breadth
of its appeal.   Yet although all three of the necessary elements appear in the play, it has more action
than passion and more passion than characterisation.   And this fact leads us to the theory, omitted
by Victor Hugo from his preface, that the mob is
more important than the women and the women
more important than the thinkers, in the average
theatre audience.   Indeed, a deeper consideration
of the subject almost leads us to discard the thinkers as a psychologic force and to obliterate the
distinction between the women and the mob.   It is
to an unthinking and feminine-minded mob that
the dramatist must first of all appeal; and this
leads us to believe that action with passion for its
motive is the prime essential for a play.

For, nowadays at least, it is most essential that the drama should appeal to a crowd of women. Practically speaking, our matinée audiences are composed entirely of women, and our evening audiences are composed chiefly of women and the men that they have brought with them. Very few men go to the theatre unattached; and these few are not important enough, from the theoretic standpoint, to alter the psychologic aspect of the audience. And it is this that constitutes one of the most important differences between a modern theatre audience and other kinds of crowds.

The influence of this fact upon the dramatist is very potent. First of all, as I have said, it forces him to deal chiefly in action with passion for its motive. And this necessity accounts for the preponderance of female characters over male in the large majority of the greatest modern plays. Notice Nora Helmer, Mrs. Alving, Hedda Gabler; notice Magda and Camille; notice Mrs. Tanqueray, Mrs. Ebbsmith, Iris, and Letty,— to cite only a few examples. Furthermore, since women are by nature comparatively inattentive, the femininity of the modern theatre audience forces the dramatist to employ the elementary technical tricks of repetition and parallelism, in order to keep his play clear, though much of it be unattended to. Eugène Scribe, who knew the theatre, used to say that every important statement in the exposition of a play must be made at least three times. This, of course, is seldom necessary in a novel, where things may be said once for all.

The prevailing inattentiveness of a theatre audience at the present day is due also to the fact that it is peculiarly conscious of itself, apart from the play that it has come to see. Many people " go to the theatre," as the phrase is, without caring much whether they see one play or another; what they want chiefly is to immerse themselves in a theatre audience. This is especially true, in New York, of the large percentage of people from out of town who " go to the theatre " merely as one phase of their metropolitan experience. It is true, also, of the many women in the boxes and the orchestra who go less to see than to be seen. It is one of the great difficulties of the dramatist that he must capture and enchain the attention of an audience thus composed. A man does not pick up a novel unless he cares to read it; but many people go to the theatre chiefly for the sense of being there. Certainly, therefore, the problem of the dramatist is, in this respect, more difficult than that of the novelist, for he must make his audience lose consciousness of itself in the consciousness of his play.

One of the most essential differences between a theatre audience and other kinds of crowds lies in the purpose for which it is convened. This pur-

pose is always recreation. A theatre audience is
therefore less serious than a church congregation
or a political or social convention. It does not
come to be edified or educated; it has no desire to
be taught: what it wants is to have its emotions
played upon. It seeks amusement — in the widest
sense of the word — amusement through laughter,
sympathy, terror, and tears. And it is amusement
of this sort that the great dramatists have ever
given it.

The trouble with most of the dreamers who
league themselves for the uplifting of the stage is
that they consider the theatre with an illogical solemnity. They base their efforts on the proposition that a theatre audience ought to want to be
edified. As a matter of fact, no audience ever does.
Molière and Shakespeare, who knew the limits of
their art, never said a word about uplifting the
stage. They wrote plays to please the crowd; and
if, through their inherent greatness, they became
teachers as well as entertainers, they did so without any tall talk about the solemnity of their
mission. Their audiences learned largely, but they
did so unawares,— God being with them when they
knew it not. The demand for an endowed theatre
in America comes chiefly from those who believe
that a great play cannot earn its own living. Yet
Hamlet has made more money than any other play
in English; *The School for Scandal* never fails

to draw; and in our own day we have seen *Cyrano de Bergerac* coining money all around the world. There were not any endowed theatres in Elizabethan London. Give the crowd the sort of plays it wants, and you will not have to seek beneficence to keep your theatre floating. But, on the other hand, no endowed theatre will ever lure the crowd to listen to the sort of plays it does not want. There is a wise maxim appended to one of Mr. George Ade's *Fables in Slang:* "In uplifting, get underneath." If the theatre in America is weak, what it needs is not endowment: it needs great and popular plays. Why should we waste our money and our energy trying to make the crowd come to see *The Master Builder*, or *A Blot in the 'Scutcheon*, or *The Hour Glass*, or *Pélléas and Mélisande?* It is willing enough to come without urging to see *Othello* and *The Second Mrs. Tanqueray*. Give us one great dramatist who understands the crowd, and we shall not have to form societies to propagate his art. Let us cease our prattle of the theatre for the few. Any play that is really great as drama will interest the many.

IV

One point remains to be considered. In any theatre audience there are certain individuals who do not belong to the crowd. They are in it, but not of it; for they fail to merge their individual self-consciousness in the general self-consciousness of the multitude. Such are the professional critics, and other confirmed frequenters of the theatre. It is not for them primarily that plays are written; and any one who has grown individualised through the theatre-going habit cannot help looking back regretfully upon those fresher days when he belonged, unthinking, to the crowd. A first-night audience is anomalous, in that it is composed largely of individuals opposed to self-surrender; and for this reason, a first-night judgment of the merits of a play is rarely final. The dramatist has written for a crowd, and he is judged by individuals. Most dramatic critics will tell you that they long to lose themselves in the crowd, and regret the aloofness from the play that comes of their profession. It is because of this aloofness of the critic that most dramatic criticism fails.

Throughout the present discussion, I have insisted on the point that the great dramatists have always written primarily for the many. Yet now I must add that when once they have fulfilled this prime necessity, they may also write secondarily for the few. And the very greatest have always done so. In so far as he was a dramatist, Shakespeare wrote for the crowd; in so far as he was a lyric poet, he wrote for himself; and in so far as he was a sage and a stylist, he wrote for the individual. In making sure of his appeal to the many, he earned the right to appeal to the few. At the thirty-cent performance of *Othello* that I spoke of, I was probably the only person present who failed to submerge his individuality beneath the common consciousness of the audience. Shakespeare made a play that could appeal to the rabble of that middle-western town; but he wrote it in a verse that none of them could hear: —

> Not poppy, nor mandragora,
> Nor all the drowsy syrups of the world,
> Shall ever medicine thee to that sweet sleep
> Which thou ow'dst yesterday.

The greatest dramatist of all, in writing for the crowd, did not neglect the individual.

III

THE ACTOR AND THE DRAMATIST

WE have already agreed that the dramatist works
ever under the sway of three influences which are not
felt by exclusively literary artists like the poet and
the novelist. The physical conditions of the theatre in any age affect to a great extent the form
and structure of the drama; the conscious or un-
conscious demands of the audience, as we have observed in the preceding chapter, determine for the
dramatist the themes he shall portray; and the
range or restrictions of his actors have an immediate effect upon the dramatist's great task of
character-creation. In fact, so potent is the influence of the actor upon the dramatist that the latter, in creating character, goes to work very differently from his literary fellow-artists,— the
novelist, the story-writer, or the poet. Great characters in non-dramatic fiction have often resulted
from abstract imagining, without direct reference
to any actual person: Don Quixote, Tito Melema,
Leatherstocking, sprang full-grown from their
creators' minds and struck the world as strange
and new. But the greatest characters in the drama

have almost always taken on the physical, and to a great extent the mental, characteristics of certain great actors for whom they have been fashioned. Cyrano is not merely Cyrano, but also Coquelin; Mascarille is not merely Mascarille, but also Molière; Hamlet is not merely Hamlet, but also Richard Burbage. Closet-students of the plays of Sophocles may miss a point or two if they fail to consider that the dramatist prepared the part of Œdipus in three successive dramas for a certain star-performer on the stage of Dionysus. The greatest dramatists have built their plays not so much for reading in the closet as for immediate presentation on the stage; they have grown to greatness only after having achieved an initial success that has given them the freedom of the theatre; and their conceptions of character have therefore crystallised around the actors that they have found waiting to present their parts. A novelist may conceive his heroine freely as being tall or short, frail or firmly built; but if a dramatist is making a play for an actress like Maude Adams, an airy, slight physique is imposed upon his heroine in advance.

Shakespeare was, among other things, the director of the Lord Chamberlain's men, who performed in the Globe, upon the Bankside; and his plays are replete with evidences of the influence upon him of the actors whom he had in charge.   It is patent, for example, that the same comedian must have created Launce in *Two Gentlemen of Verona* and Launcelot Gobbo in the *Merchant of Venice;* the low comic hit of one production was bodily repeated in the next. It is almost as obvious that the parts of Mercutio and Gratiano must have been intrusted to the same performer; both characters seem made to fit the same histrionic temperament. If Hamlet were the hero of a novel, we should all, I think, conceive of him as slender, and the author would agree with us; yet, in the last scene of the play, the Queen expressly says, " He's fat, and scant of breath." This line has puzzled many commentators, as seeming out of character; but it merely indicates that Richard Burbage was fleshy during the season of 1602.

The Elizabethan expedient of disguising the heroine as a boy, which was invented by John Lyly, made popular by Robert Greene, and eagerly adopted by Shakespeare and Fletcher, seems unconvincing on the modern stage. It is hard for us to imagine how Orlando can fail to recognise his love when he meets her clad as Ganymede in the forest of Arden, or how Bassanio can be blinded to the figure of his wife when she enters the courtroom in the almost feminine robes of a doctor of laws. Clothes cannot make a man out of an actress; we recognize Ada Rehan or Julia Marlowe beneath the trappings and the suits of their dis-

guises; and it might seem that Shakespeare was
depending over-much upon the proverbial credulity of theatre audiences.   But a glance at histrionic conditions in Shakespeare's day will show us
immediately why he used this expedient of disguise
not only for Portia and Rosalind, but for Viola
and Imogen as well.   Shakespeare wrote these
parts to be played not by women but by boys.
Now, when a boy playing a woman disguised himself as a woman playing a boy, the disguise must
have seemed baffling, not only to Orlando and Bassanio on the stage, but also to the audience.   It
was Shakespeare's boy actors, rather than his narrative imagination, that made him recur repeatedly
in this case to a dramatic expedient which he would
certainly discard if he were writing for actresses
to-day.

If we turn from the work of Shakespeare to that
of Molière, we shall find many more evidences of
the influence of the actor on the dramatist.   In
fact, Molière's entire scheme of character-creation
cannot be understood without direct reference to
the histrionic capabilities of the various members
of the *Troupe de Monsieur*.   Molière's immediate
and practical concern was not so much to create
comic characters for all time as to make effective
parts for La Grange and Du Croisy and Magdeleine Béjart, for his wife and for himself.   La
Grange seems to have been the Charles Wyndham

of his day,— every inch a gentleman; his part in any of the plays may be distinguished by its elegant urbanity. In *Les Précieuses Ridicules* the gentlemanly characters are actually named La Grange and Du Croisy; the actors walked on and played themselves; it is as if Augustus Thomas had called the hero of his best play, not Jack Brookfield, but John Mason. In the early period of Molière's art, before he broadened as an actor, the parts that he wrote for himself were often so much alike from play to play that he called them by the same conventional theatric name of Mascarille or Sganarelle, and played them, doubtless, with the same costume and make-up. Later on, when he became more versatile as an actor, he wrote for himself a wider range of parts and individualised them in name as well as in nature. His growth in depicting the characters of young women is curiously coincident with the growth of his wife as an actress for whom to devise such characters. Molière's best woman — Célimène, in *Le Misanthrope* — was created for Mlle. Molière at the height of her career, and is endowed with all her physical and mental traits.

The reason why so many of the Queen Anne dramatists in England wrote comedies setting forth a dandified and foppish gentleman is that Colley Cibber, the foremost actor of the time, could play the fop better than he could play anything else.

The reason why there is no love scene between
Charles Surface and Maria in *The School for
Scandal* is that Sheridan knew that the actor and
the actress who were cast for these respective roles
were incapable of making love gracefully upon
the stage. The reason why Victor Hugo's *Cromwell* overleaped itself in composition and became
impossible for purposes of stage production is that
Talma, for whom the character of Cromwell was
designed, died before the piece was finished, and
Hugo, despairing of having the part adequately
acted, completed the play for the closet instead of
for the stage. But it is unnecessary to cull from
the past further instances of the direct dependence
of the dramatist upon his actors. We have only
to look about us at the present day to see the same
influence at work.

For example, the career of one of the very best
endowed theatrical composers of the nineteenth
century, the late Victorien Sardou, has been molded
and restricted for all time by the talents of a single star performer, Mme. Sarah Bernhardt. Under the influence of Eugène Scribe, Sardou began
his career at the Théatre Français with a wide
range of well-made plays, varying in scope from
the social satire of *Nos Intimes* and the farcical in-
trigue of *Les Pattes de Mouche* (known to us in
English as *The Scrap of Paper*) to the tremendous
historic panorama of *Patrie*. When Sarah Bern-

hardt left the Comédie Française, Sardou followed
in her footsteps, and afterwards devoted most of
his energy to preparing a series of melodramas to
serve successively as vehicles for her.   Now, Sarah
Bernhardt is an actress of marked abilities, and
limitations likewise marked.   In sheer perfection
of technique she surpasses all performers of her
time.   She is the acme of histrionic dexterity; all
that she does upon the stage is, in sheer effectiveness, superb.   But in her work she has no soul;
she lacks the sensitive sweet lure of Duse, the serene
and star-lit poetry of Modjeska.   Three things she
does supremely well.   She can be seductive, with a
cooing voice; she can be vindictive, with a cawing
voice; and, voiceless, she can die.   Hence the formula of Sardou's melodramas.

His heroines are almost always Sarah Bern-
hardts,— luring, tremendous, doomed to die.
Fédora, Gismonda, La Tosca, Zoraya, are but a
single woman who transmigrates from play to
play.   We find her in different countries and in
different times; but she always lures and fascinates
a man, storms against insuperable circumstance,
coos and caws, and in the outcome dies.   One of
Sardou's latest efforts, *La Sorcière*, presents the
dry bones of the formula without the flesh and
blood of life.   Zoraya appears first shimmering
in moonlight upon the hills of Spain,— dovelike
in voice, serpentining in seductiveness.   Next, she

is allowed to hypnotise the audience while she is hypnotising the daughter of the governor. She is loved and she is lost. She curses the high tribunal of the Inquisition,— a dove no longer now. And she dies upon cathedral steps, to organ music. *The Sorceress* is but a lifeless piece of mechanism; and when it was performed in English by Mrs. Patrick Campbell, it failed to lure or to thrill. But Sarah Bernhardt, because as an actress she *is* Zoraya, contrived to lift it into life. Justly we may say that, in a certain sense, this is Sarah Bernhardt's drama instead of Victorien Sardou's. With her, it is a play; without her, it is nothing but a formula. The young author of *Patrie* promised better things than this. Had he chosen, he might have climbed to nobler heights. But he chose instead to write, year after year, a vehicle for the Muse of Melodrama, and sold his laurel crown for gate-receipts.

If Sardou suffered through playing the sedulous ape to a histrionic artist, it is no less true that the same practice has been advantageous to M. Edmond Rostand. M. Rostand has shrewdly written for the greatest comedian of the recent generation; and Constant Coquelin was the making of him as a dramatist. The poet's early pieces, like *Les Romanesques*, disclosed him as a master of preciosity, exquisitely lyrical, but lacking in the sterner stuff of drama. He seemed a new de Ban-

ville — dainty, dallying, and deft — a writer of
witty and pretty verses — nothing more.   Then
it fell to his lot to devise an acting part for Coquelin, which in the compass of a single play should
allow that great performer to sweep through the
whole wide range of his varied and versatile accomplishment.   With the figure of Coquelin before him,
M. Rostand set earnestly to work.   The result of
his endeavor was the character of Cyrano de Bergerac, which is considered by many critics the
richest acting part, save Hamlet, in the history of
the theatre.

L'Aiglon was also devised under the immediate
influence of the same actor.   The genesis of this
latter play is, I think, of peculiar interest to students of the drama; and I shall therefore relate
it at some length.   The facts were told by M.
Coquelin himself to his friend Professor Brander
Matthews, who has kindly permitted me to state
them in this place.   One evening, after the extraordinary success of *Cyrano*, M. Rostand met
Coquelin at the Porte St. Martin and said, " You
know, Coq, this is not the last part I want to write
for you.   Can't you give me an idea to get me
started — an idea for another character? "   The
actor thought for a moment, and then answered,
" I've always wanted to play a *vieux grognard du
premier empire — un grenadier à grandes moustaches.*"   .   .   .   A grumpy grenadier of Napo-

leon's army — a grenadier with sweeping moustaches — with this cue the dramatist set to work and gradually imagined the character of Flambeau. He soon saw that if the great Napoleon were to appear in the play he would dominate the action and steal the centre of the stage from the soldier-hero. He therefore decided to set the story after the Emperor's death, in the time of the weak and vacillating Duc de Reichstadt. Flambeau, who had served the eagle, could now transfer his allegiance to the eaglet, and stand dominant with the memory of battles that had been. But after the dramatist had been at work upon the play for some time, he encountered the old difficulty in a new guise. At last he came in despair to Coquelin and said, " It isn't your play, Coq; it can't be; the young duke is running away with it, and I can't stop him; Flambeau is but a secondary figure after all. What shall I do? " And Coquelin, who understood him, answered, " Take it to Sarah; she has just played Hamlet, and wants to do another boy." So M. Rostand " took it to Sarah," and finished up the duke with her in view, while in the background the figure of Flambeau scowled upon him over *grandes moustaches* — a true *grognard* indeed! Thus it happened that Coquelin never played the part of Flambeau until he came to New York with Mme. Sarah Bernhardt in the fall of 1900; and the grenadier conceived in the Porte St.

Martin first saw the footlights in the Garden Theatre.

But the contemporary English-speaking stage furnishes examples just as striking of the influence of the actor on the dramatist. Sir Arthur Wing Pinero's greatest heroine, Paula Tanqueray, wore from her inception the physical aspect of Mrs. Patrick Campbell. Many of the most effective dramas of Mr. Henry Arthur Jones have been built around the personality of Sir Charles Wyndham. The Wyndham part in Mr. Jones's plays is always a gentleman of the world, who understands life because he has lived it, and is " wise with the quiet memory of old pain." He is moral because he knows the futility of immorality. He is lonely, lovable, dignified, reliable, and sound. By serene and unobtrusive understanding he straightens out the difficulties in which the other people of the play have wilfully become entangled. He shows them the error of their follies, preaches a worldly-wise little sermon to each one, and sends them back to their true places in life, sadder and wiser men and women. In order to give Sir Charles Wyndham an opportunity to display all phases of his experienced gentility in such a character as this, Mr. Jones has repeated the part in drama after drama.

Many of the greatest characters of the theatre have been so essentially imbued with the physical and mental personality of the actors who created them that they have died with their performers and been lost forever after from the world of art. In this regard we think at once of Rip Van Winkle. The little play that Mr. Jefferson, with the aid of Dion Boucicault, fashioned out of Washington Irving's story is scarcely worth the reading; and if, a hundred years from now, any student of the drama happens to look it over, he may wonder in vain why it was so beloved, for many, many years, by all America; and there will come no answer, since the actor's art will then be only a tale that is told. So Beau Brummel died with Mr. Mansfield; and if our children, who never saw his superb performance, chance in future years to read the lines of Mr. Fitch's play, they will hardly believe us when we tell them that the character of Brummel once was great. With such current instances before us, it ought not to be so difficult as many university professors find it to understand the vogue of certain plays of the Elizabethan and Restoration eras which seem to us now, in the reading, lifeless things. When we study the mad dramas of Nat Lee, we should remember Betterton; and properly to appreciate Thomas Otway, we must imagine the aspect and the voice of Elizabeth Barry.

It may truthfully be said that Mrs. Barry created Otway, both as dramatist and poet; for *The Orphan* and *Venice Preserved,* the two most pathetic plays in English, would never have been written but for her.   It is often thus within the power of an actor to create a dramatist; and his surest means of immortality is to inspire the composition of plays which may survive his own demise.   After Duse is dead, poets may read *La Città Morta*, and imagine her.   The memory of Coquelin is, in this way, likely to live longer than that of Talma. We can merely guess at Talma's art, because the plays in which he acted are unreadable to-day. But if M. Rostand's *Cyrano* is read a hundred years from now, it will be possible for students of it to imagine in detail the salient features of the art of Coquelin.   It will be evident to them that the actor made love luringly and died effectively, that he was capable of lyric reading and staccato gasconade, that he had a burly humor and that touch of sentiment that trembles into tears.   Similarly we know to-day, from the fact that Shakespeare played the Ghost in *Hamlet*, that he must have had a voice that was full and resonant and deep.   So from reading the plays of Molière we can imagine the robust figure of Magdeleine Béjart, the grace of La Grange, the pretty petulance of the flighty fair Armande.

Some sense of this must have been in the mind of Sir Henry Irving when he strove industriously to create a dramatist who might survive him and immortalise his memory.   The facile, uncreative

Wills was granted many chances, and in *Charles I* lost an opportunity to make a lasting drama. Lord Tennyson came near the mark in *Becket;* but this play, like those of Wills, has not proved sturdy enough to survive the actor who inspired it.   For all his striving, Sir Henry left no dramatist as a monument to his art.

IV

STAGE CONVENTIONS IN MODERN TIMES

In 1581 Sir Philip Sidney praised the tragedy of *Gorboduc*, which he had seen acted by the gentlemen of the Inner Temple, because it was " full of stately speeches and well-sounding phrases." A few years later the young poet, Christopher Marlowe, promised the audience of his initial tragedy that they should " hear the Scythian Tamburlaine threatening the world with high astounding terms." These two statements are indicative of the tenor of Elizabethan plays. *Gorboduc*, to be sure, was a ponderous piece, made according to the pseudo-classical fashion that soon went out of favor; while *Tamburlaine the Great* was triumphant with the drums and tramplings of romance. The two plays were diametrically opposed in method; but they had this in common: each was full of stately speeches and of high astounding terms.

Nearly a century later, in 1670, John Dryden

added to the second part of his *Conquest of Granada* an epilogue in which he criticised adversely the dramatists of the elder age.   Speaking of Ben Jonson and his contemporaries, he said:

> But were they now to write, when critics weigh
> Each line, and every word, throughout a play,
> None of them, no, not Jonson in his height,
> Could pass without allowing grains for weight.
>
> .   .   .   .
>
> Wit 's now arrived to a more high degree;
> Our native language more refined and free:
> Our ladies and our men now speak more wit
> In conversation than those poets writ.

This criticism was characteristic of a new era that was dawning in the English drama, during which a playwright could hope for no greater glory than to be praised for the brilliancy of his dialogue or the smartness of his repartee.

At the present day, if you ask the average theatre-goer about the merits of the play that he has lately witnessed, he will praise it not for its stately speeches nor its clever repartee, but because its presentation was " so natural." He will tell you that *A Woman's Way* gave an apt and admirable reproduction of contemporary manners in New York; he will mention the make of the automobile that went chug-chugging off the stage at the second curtain-fall of *Man and Superman*, or he will assure you that *Lincoln* made him feel the very presence of the martyred President his father actually saw.

These different classes of comments give evidence of three distinct steps in the evolution of the English drama. During the sixteenth and seventeenth centuries it was essentially a Drama of Rhetoric; throughout the eighteenth century it was mainly a Drama of Conversation; and during the nineteenth century it has grown to be a Drama of Illusion. During the first period it aimed at poetic power, during the second at brilliancy of dialogue, and during the third at naturalness of representment. Throughout the last three centuries, the gradual perfecting of the physical conditions of the theatre has made possible the Drama of Illusion; the conventions of the actor's art have undergone a similar progression; and at the same time the change in the taste of the theatre-going public has made a well-sustained illusion a condition precedent to success upon the modern stage.

II

Mr. Ben Greet, in his sceneless performances of Shakespeare during recent seasons, has reminded us of some of the main physical features of the Elizabethan theatre; and the others are so generally known that we need review them only briefly. A typical Elizabethan play-house, like the Globe or the Blackfriars, stood roofless in the air. The stage was a projecting platform surrounded on three sides by the groundlings who had paid threepence for the privilege of standing in the pit; and around this pit, or yard, were built boxes for the city madams and the gentlemen of means. Often the side edges of the stage itself were lined with young gallants perched on three-legged stools, who twitted the actors when they pleased or disturbed the play by boisterous interruptions. At the back of the platform was hung an arras through which the players entered, and which could be drawn aside to discover a set piece of stage furnishing, like a bed or a banqueting board. Above the arras was built an upper room, which might serve as Juliet's balcony or as the speaking-place of a commandant supposed to stand upon a city's walls. No scenery was employed, except some elaborate properties that might be drawn on and off before the eyes of the spectators, like the trellised arbor in *The Spanish Tragedy* on which the young Horatio was hanged. Since there was no curtain, the actors could never be " discovered " on the stage and were forced to make an exit at the end of every scene. Plays were produced by daylight, under the sun of afternoon; and the stage could not be darkened, even when it was necessary for Macbeth to perpetrate a midnight murder.

In order to succeed in a theatre such as this, the drama was necessarily forced to be a Drama of Rhetoric. From 1576, when James Burbage built the first play-house in London, until 1642, when the theatres were formally closed by act of Parliament, the drama dealt with stately speeches and with high astounding terms. It was played upon a platform, and had to appeal more to the ears of the audience than to their eyes. Spectacular elements it had to some extent,— gaudy, though inappropriate, costumes, and stately processions across the stage; but no careful imitation of the actual facts of life, no illusion of reality in the representment, could possibly be effected.

The absence of scenery forced the dramatists of the time to introduce poetic passages to suggest the atmosphere of their scenes. Lorenzo and Jessica opened the last act of *The Merchant of Venice* with a pretty dialogue descriptive of a moonlit evening, and the banished duke in *As You Like It* discoursed at length upon the pleasures of life in the forest. The stage could not be darkened in *Macbeth;* but the hero was made to say, " Light thickens, and the crow makes wing to the rooky wood." Sometimes, when the scene was supposed to change from one country to another, a chorus was sent forth, as in *Henry V,* to ask the audience frankly to transfer their imaginations overseas.

The fact that the stage was surrounded on three sides by standing spectators forced the actor to emulate the platform orator. Set speeches were introduced bodily into the text of a play, although they impeded the progress of the action. Jacques reined a comedy to a standstill while he discoursed at length upon the seven ages of man. Soliloquies were common, and formal dialogues prevailed. By convention, all characters, regardless of their education or station in life, were considered capable of talking not only verse, but poetry. The untutored sea-captain in *Twelfth Night* spoke of "Arion on the dolphin's back," and in another play the sapheads Salanio and Salarino discoursed most eloquent music.

In New York at the present day a singular similarity to Elizabethan conventions may be noted in the Chinese theatre in Doyer Street. Here we have a platform drama in all its nakedness. There is no curtain, and the stage is bare of scenery. The musicians sit upon the stage, and the actors enter through an arras at the right or at the left of the rear wall. The costumes are elaborate, and the players frequently parade around the stage. Long speeches and set colloquies are common. Only the crudest properties are used. Two candlesticks and a small image on a table are taken to represent a temple; a man seated upon an overturned chair is supposed to be a general on a

charger; and when a character is obliged to cross a
river, he walks the length of the stage trailing an
oar behind him. The audience does not seem to
notice that these conventions are unnatural,— any
more than did the 'prentices in the pit, when
Burbage, with the sun shining full upon his face,
announced that it was then the very witching time
of night.

The Drama of Rhetoric which was demanded by
the physical conditions of the Elizabethan stage
survived the Restoration and did not die until the
day of Addison's *Cato*. Imitations of it have
even struggled on the stage within the nineteenth
century. The *Virginius* of Sheridan Knowles and
the *Richelieu* of Bulwer-Lytton were both framed
upon the Elizabethan model, and carried the platform drama down to recent times. But though
traces of the platform drama still exist, the period
of its pristine vigor terminated with the closing of
the theatres in 1642.

When the drama was resumed in 1660, the physical conditions of the theatre underwent a material
change. At this time two great play-houses were
chartered,— the King's Theatre in Drury Lane,
and the Duke of York's Theatre in Lincoln's Inn
Fields. Thomas Killigrew, the manager of the
Theatre Royal, was the first to introduce women
actors on the stage; and parts which formerly had
been played by boys were soon performed by

actresses as moving as the great Elizabeth Barry. To William Davenant, the manager of the Duke's Theatre, belongs the credit for a still more important innovation. During the eighteen years when public dramatic performances had been prohibited, he had secured permission now and then to produce an opera upon a private stage. For these musical entertainments he took as a model the masques, or court celebrations, which had been the most popular form of private theatricals in the days of Elizabeth and James. It is well known that masques had been produced with elaborate scenic appointments even at a time when the professional stage was bare of scenery. While the theatres had been closed, Davenant had used scenery in his operas, to keep them out of the forbidden pale of professional plays; and now in 1660, when he came forth as a regular theatre manager, he continued to use scenery, and introduced it into the production of comedies and tragedies.

But the use of scenery was not the only innovation that carried the Restoration theatre far beyond its Elizabethan prototype. Play-houses were now regularly roofed; and the stage was artificially lighted by lamps. The shifting of scenery demanded the use of a curtain; and it became possible for the first time to disclose actors upon the stage and to leave them grouped before the audience at the end of an act.

All of these improvements rendered possible a closer approach to naturalness of representment than had ever been made before. Palaces and flowered meads, drawing-rooms and city streets, could now be suggested by actual scenery instead of by descriptive passages in the text. Costumes became appropriate, and properties were more nicely chosen to give a flavor of actuality to the scene. At the same time the platform receded, and the groundlings no longer stood about it on the sides. The gallants were banished from the stage, and the greater part of the audience was gathered directly in front of the actors. Some traces of the former platform system, however, still remained. In front of the curtain, the stage projected into a wide " apron," as it was called, lined on either side by boxes filled with spectators; and the house was so inadequately lighted that almost all the acting had to be done within the focus of the footlights. After the curtain rose, the actors advanced into this projecting " apron " and performed the main business of the act beyond the range of scenery and furniture.

With the " apron " stage arose a more natural form of play than had been produced upon the Elizabethan platform. The Drama of Rhetoric was soon supplanted by the Drama of Conversation. Oratory gradually disappeared, set speeches were abolished, and poetic lines gave place to rapid repartee. The comedy of conversation that began with Sir George Etherege in 1664 reached its culmination with Sheridan in a little more than a hundred years; and during this century the drama became more and more natural as the years progressed. Even in the days of Sheridan, however, the conventions of the theatre were still essentially unreal. An actor entered a room by walking through the walls; stage furniture was formally arranged; and each act terminated with the players grouped in a semicircle and bowing obeisance to applause. The lines in Sheridan's comedies were indiscriminately witty. Every character, regardless of his birth or education, had his clever things to say; and the servant bandied epigrams with the lord.

It was not until the nineteenth century was well under way that a decided improvement was made in the physical conditions of the theatre. When Madame Vestris assumed the management of the Olympic Theatre in London in 1831 she inaugurated a new era in stage conventions. Her husband, Charles James Mathews, says in his autobiography, " There was introduced that reform in all theatrical matters which has since been adopted in every theatre in the kingdom. Drawing-rooms were fitted up like drawing-rooms and furnished with care and taste. Two chairs no longer indicated that two persons were to be seated, the two chairs being removed indicating that the two persons were *not* to be seated." At the first performance of Boucicault's *London Assurance,* in 1841, a further innovation was marked by the introduction of the " box set," as it is called. Instead of representing an interior scene by a series of wings set one behind the other, the scene-shifters now built the side walls of a room solidly from front to rear; and the actors were made to enter, not by walking through the wings, but by opening real doors that turned upon their hinges. At the same time, instead of the formal stage furniture of former years, appointments were introduced that were carefully designed to suit the actual conditions of the room to be portrayed. From this time stage-settings advanced rapidly to greater and greater degrees of naturalness. Acting, however, was still largely conventional; for the " apron " stage survived, with its semicircle of footlights, and every important piece of stage business had to be done within their focus.

The greatest revolution of modern times in stage conventions owes its origin directly to the invention of the electric light. Now that it is possible to make every corner of the stage clearly visible from all parts of the house, it is no longer necessary for an actor to hold the centre of the scene. The introduction of electric lights abolished the necessity of the " apron " stage and made possible the picture-frame proscenium; and the removal of the " apron " struck the death-blow to the Drama of Conversation and led directly to the Drama of Illusion.   As soon as the picture-frame proscenium was adopted, the audience demanded a picture to be placed within the frame.   The stage became essentially pictorial, and began to be used to represent faithfully the actual facts of life.   Now for the first time was realised the graphic value of the curtain-fall.   It became customary to ring the curtain down upon a picture that summed up in itself the entire dramatic accomplishment of the scene, instead of terminating an act with a general exodus of the performers or with a semicircle of bows.

The most extraordinary advances in natural stage-settings have been made within the memory of the present generation of theatre-goers.   Sunsets and starlit skies, moonlight rippling over moving waves, fires that really burn, windows of actual glass, fountains plashing with real water, — all of the naturalistic devices of the latter-day Drama of Illusion have been developed in the last few decades.

III

Acting in Elizabethan days was a presentative, rather than a representative, art.   The actor was always an actor, and absorbed his part in himself rather than submerging himself in his part. Magnificence rather than appropriateness of costume was desired by the platform actor of the Drama of Rhetoric. He wished all eyes to be directed to himself, and never desired to be considered merely as a component part of a great stage picture. Actors at that time were often robustious, periwig-pated fellows who sawed the air with their hands and tore a passion to tatters.

With the rapid development of the theatre after the Restoration, came a movement toward greater naturalness in the conventions of acting. The player in the " apron " of a Queen Anne stage resembled a drawing-room entertainer rather than a platform orator. Fine gentlemen and ladies in the boxes that lined the " apron " applauded the witticisms of Sir Courtly Nice or Sir Fopling Flutter, as if they themselves were partakers in the conversation. Actors like Colley Cibber acquired a great reputation for their natural representment of the manners of polite society.

The Drama of Conversation, therefore, was acted with more natural conventions than the Drama of Rhetoric that had preceded it. And yet we find that Charles Lamb, in criticising the old actors of the eighteenth century, praises them for the essential unreality of their presentations. They carried the spectator far away from the actual world to a region where society was more splendid and careless and brilliant and lax. They did not aim to produce an illusion of naturalness as our actors do to-day. If we compare the old-style acting of *The School for Scandal*, that is described in the essays of Lamb, with the modern performance of *Sweet Kitty Bellairs*, which dealt with the same period, we shall see at once how modern acting has grown less presentative and more representative than it was in the days of Bensley and Bannister.

The Drama of Rhetoric and the Drama of Conversation both struggled on in sporadic survivals throughout the first half of the nineteenth century; and during this period the methods of the platform actor and the parlor actor were consistently maintained. The actor of the " old school," as we are now fond of calling him, was compelled by the physical conditions of the theatre to keep within the focus of the footlights, and therefore in close proximity to the spectators. He could take the audience into his confidence more readily than can the player of the present. Sometimes even now an actor steps out of the picture in order to talk intimately with the audience; but usually at the present day it is customary for actors to seem totally oblivious of the spectators and remain always within the picture on the stage. The actor of the " old school " was fond of the long speeches of the Drama of Rhetoric and the

brilliant lines of the Drama of Conversation. It
may be remembered that the old actor in *Trelawny
of the Wells* condemned a new-style play because
it didn't contain "what you could really call a
speech." He wanted what the French term a
tirade to exercise his lungs and split the ears of
the groundlings.

But with the growth of the Drama of Illusion,
produced within a picture-frame proscenium, actors
have come to recognise and apply the maxim,
"Actions speak louder than words." What an
actor *does* is now considered more important than
what he *says*. The most powerful moment in Mrs.
Fiske's performance of *Hedda Gabler* was the
minute or more in the last act when she remained
absolutely silent. This moment was worth a dozen
of the "real speeches" that were sighed for by the
old actor in *Trelawny*. Few of those who saw
James A. Herne in *Shore Acres* will forget the
impressive close of the play. The stage represented the living-room of a homely country-house,
with a large open fireplace at one side. The night
grew late; and one by one the characters retired,
until at last old Nathaniel Berry was left alone
upon the stage. Slowly he locked the doors and
closed the windows and put all things in order for
the night. Then he took a candle and went up-
stairs to bed, leaving the room empty and dark
except for the flaming of the fire on the hearth.

Great progress toward naturalness in contemporary acting has been occasioned by the disappearance of the soliloquy and the aside. The relinquishment of these two time-honored expedients has been accomplished only in most recent times. Sir Arthur Pinero's early farces abounded with asides and even lengthy soliloquies; but his later plays are made entirely without them. The present prevalence of objection to both is due largely to the strong influence of Ibsen's rigid dramaturgic structure. Dramatists have become convinced that the soliloquy and the aside are lazy expedients, and that with a little extra labor the most complicated plot may be developed without resort to either. The passing of the aside has had an important effect on naturalness of acting. In speaking a line audible to the audience but supposed to be unheard by the other characters on the stage, an actor was forced by the very nature of the speech to violate the illusion of the stage picture by stepping out of the frame, as it were, in order to take the audience into his confidence. Not until the aside was abolished did it become possible for an actor to follow the modern rule of seeming totally oblivious of his audience.

There is less logical objection to the soliloquy, however; and I am inclined to think that the present avoidance of it is overstrained. Stage soliloquies are of two kinds, which we may call for convenience the constructive and the reflective. By a constructive soliloquy we mean one introduced arbitrarily to explain the progress of the plot, like that at the beginning of the last act of *Lady Windermere's Fan,* in which the heroine frankly tells the audience what she has been thinking and doing between the acts. By a reflective soliloquy we mean one like those of *Hamlet,* in which the audience is given merely a revelation of a train of personal thought or emotion, and in which the dramatist makes no utilitarian reference to the structure of the plot. The constructive soliloquy is as undesirable as the aside, because it forces the actor out of the stage picture in exactly the same way; but a good actor may easily read a reflective soliloquy without seeming in the least unnatural.

Modern methods of lighting, as we have seen, have carried the actor away from the centre of the stage, so that now important business is often done far from the footlights. This tendency has led to further innovations. Actors now frequently turn their backs to the audience,— a thing unheard of before the advent of the Drama of Illusion; and frequently, also, they do their most effective work at moments when they have no lines to speak.

But the present tendency toward naturalness of representment has, to some extent, exaggerated the importance of stage-management even at the expense of acting. A successful play by Clyde Fitch

usually owed its popularity, not so much to the
excellence of the acting as to the careful attention
of the author to the most minute details of the
stage picture. Fitch could make an act out of a
wedding or a funeral, a Cook's tour or a steamer
deck, a bed or an automobile. The extraordinary
cleverness and accuracy of his observation of those
petty details that make life a thing of shreds and
patches were all that distinguished his method from
that of the melodramatist who makes a scene out
of a buzz-saw or a waterfall, a locomotive or a
ferryboat. Oftentimes the contemporary playwright follows the method suggested by Mr. Crum-
mles to Nicholas Nickleby, and builds his piece
around " a real pump and two washing-tubs." At
a certain moment in the second act of *The Girl of
the Golden West* the wind-storm was the real actor
in the scene, and the hero and the heroine were but
mutes or audience to the act.

This emphasis of stage illusion is fraught with
certain dangers to the art of acting. In the modern picture-play the lines themselves are often of
such minor importance that the success or failure
of the piece depends little on the reading of the
words. Many young actors, therefore, cannot get
that rigid training in the art of reading which
could be secured in the stock companies of the generation past. Poor reading is the one great weakness of contemporary acting. I can think of only

one actor on the American stage to-day whose reading of both prose and verse is always faultless.
I mean Mr. Otis Skinner, who secured his early
training playing minor parts with actors of the
" old school." It has become possible, under present conditions, for young actresses ignorant of elo-
cution and unskilled in the first principles of im-
personation to be exploited as stars merely because
of their personal charm. A beautiful young
woman, whether she can act or not, may easily
appear " natural " in a society play, especially
written around her; and the public, lured by a pair
of eyes or a head of hair, is made as blind as love
to the absence of histrionic art. When the great
Madame Modjeska last appeared at the Fifth
Avenue Theatre, presenting some of the most wonderful plays that the world has ever seen, she
played to empty houses, while the New York public
was flocking to see some new slip of a girl seem
" natural " on the stage and appear pretty behind
the picture-frame proscenium.

IV

A comparison of an Elizabethan audience
with a theatre-full of people at the present day is,
in many ways, disadvantageous to the latter.
With our forefathers, theatre-going was an exercise in the lovely art of " making-believe." They
were told that it was night and they forgot the

sunlight; their imaginations swept around England to the trampling of armored kings, or were whisked away at a word to that Bohemia which is a desert country by the sea; and while they looked upon a platform of bare boards, they breathed the sweet air of the Forest of Arden. They needed no scenery by Alma-Tadema to make them think themselves in Rome. "What country, friends, is this?", asked Viola. "This is Illyria, lady." And the boys in the pit scented the keen, salt air and heard the surges crashing on the rocky shore.

Nowadays elaborateness of stage illusion has made spoiled children of us all. We must have a doll with real hair, or else we cannot play at being mothers. We have been pampered with mechanical toys until we have lost the art of playing without them. Where have our imaginations gone, that we must have real rain upon the stage? Shall we clamor for real snow before long, that must be kept in cold storage against the spring season? A longing for concreteness has befogged our fantasy. Even so excellent an actor as Mr. Forbes-Robertson cannot read the great speech beginning, "Look here, upon this picture and on this," in which Hamlet obviously refers to two imaginary portraits in his mind's eye, without pointing successively to two absurd caricatures that are daubed upon the scenery.

The theatre has grown older since the days when

Burbage recited that same speech upon a bare
platform; but I am not entirely sure that it has
grown wiser.   We theatre-goers have come to man-
hood and have put away childish things; but there
was a sweetness about the naïveté of childhood that
we can never quite regain.   No longer do we dream
ourselves in a garden of springtide blossoms; we
can only look upon canvas trees and paper flowers.
No longer are we charmed away to that imagined
spot where journeys end in lovers' meeting; we
can only look upon love in a parlor and notice
that the furniture is natural.   No longer do we
harken to the rich resonance of the Drama of
Rhetoric; no longer do our minds kindle with the
brilliant epigrams of the Drama of Conversation.
Good reading is disappearing from the stage; and
in its place we are left the devices of the stage-
carpenter.

It would be absurd to deny that modern stage-
craft has made possible in the theatre many excellent effects that were not dreamt of in the philosophy of Shakespeare.   Sir Arthur Pinero's
plays are better made than those of the Elizabethans, and in a narrow sense hold the mirror up to
nature more successfully than theirs.   But our
latter-day fondness for natural representment has
afflicted us with one tendency that the Elizabethans
were luckily without.   In our desire to imitate the
actual facts of life, we sometimes become near-

sighted and forget the larger truths that underlie them. We give our plays a definite date by founding them on passing fashions; we make them of an age, not for all time. We discuss contemporary social problems on the stage instead of the eternal verities lodged deep in the general heart of man. We have outgrown our pristine simplicity, but we have not yet arrived at the age of wisdom. Perhaps when playgoers have progressed for another century or two, they may discard some of the trappings and the suits of our present drama, and become again like little children.

V

ECONOMY OF ATTENTION IN THEATRICAL PERFORMANCES

I

According to the late Herbert Spencer, the sole source of force in writing is an ability to economise the attention of the reader. The word should be a window to the thought and should transmit it as transparently as possible. He says, toward the beginning of his *Philosophy of Style:*

A reader or listener has at each moment but a limited amount of mental power available. To recognise and interpret the symbols presented to him requires a part of this power; to arrange and combine the images suggested requires a further part; and only that part which remains can be used for realising the thought conveyed. Hence, the more time and attention it takes to receive and understand each sentence, the less time and attention can be given to the contained idea; and the less vividly will that idea be conveyed.

Spencer drew his illustrations of this principle mainly from the literature of the library; but its application is even more important in the literature of the stage. So many and so diverse are the elements of a theatrical performance that, unless the

attention of the spectator is attracted at every moment to the main dramatic purpose of the scene,
he will sit wide-eyed, like a child at a three-ring
circus, with his mind fluttering from point to point
and his interest dispersed and scattered. A perfect theatrical performance must harmonise the
work of many men. The dramatist, the actors
main and minor, the stage-manager, the scene-
painter, the costumer, the leader of the orchestra,
must all contribute their separate talents to the
production of a single work of art. It follows
that a nice adjustment of parts, a discriminating
subordination of minor elements to major, is absolutely necessary in order that the attention of the
audience may be focused at every moment upon
the central meaning of the scene. If the spectator
looks at scenery when he should be listening to
lines, if his attention is startled by some unexpected device of stage-management at a time when
he ought to be looking at an actor's face, or if
his mind is kept for a moment uncertain of the
most emphatic feature of a scene, the main effect
is lost and that part of the performance is a
failure.

It may be profitable to notice some of the technical devices by which attention is economised in the
theatre and the interest of the audience is thereby
centred upon the main business of the moment. In
particular it is important to observe how a scat-

tering of attention is avoided; how, when many things are shown at once upon the stage, it is possible to make an audience look at one and not observe the others.   We shall consider the subject from the point of view of the dramatist, from that of the actor, and from that of the stage-manager.

II

The dramatist, in writing, labors under a disadvantage that is not suffered by the novelist.   If a passage in a novel is not perfectly clear at the first glance, the reader may always turn back the pages and read the scene again; but on the stage a line once spoken can never be recalled.   When, therefore, an important point is to be set forth, the dramatist cannot afford to risk his clearness upon a single line.   This is particularly true in the beginning of a play.   When the curtain rises, there is always a fluttering of programs and a buzz of unfinished conversation.   Many spectators come in late and hide the stage from those behind them while they are taking off their wraps.   Consequently, most dramatists, in the preliminary exposition that must always start a play, contrive to state every important fact at least three times: first, for the attentive; second, for the intelligent; and third, for the large mass that may have missed the first two statements.   Of course, the method of presentment must be very deftly varied, in order that the artifice may not appear; but this simple rule of three is almost always practised. It was used with rare effect by Eugène Scribe, who, although he was too clever to be great, contributed more than any other writer of the nineteenth century to the science of making a modern play.

In order that the attention of the audience may not be unduly distracted by any striking effect, the dramatist must always prepare for such an effect in advance, and give the spectators an idea of what they may expect. The extraordinary nose of Cyrano de Bergerac is described at length by Ragueneau before the hero comes upon the stage. If the ugly-visaged poet should enter without this preliminary explanation, the whole effect would be lost. The spectators would nudge each other and whisper half aloud, " Look at his nose! What *is* the matter with his face? ", and would be less than half attentive to the lines. Before Lady Macbeth is shown walking in her sleep and wringing her hands that are sullied with the damned spot that all great Neptune's ocean could not wash away, her doctor and her waiting gentlewoman are sent to tell the audience of her " slumbery agitation." Thus, at the proper moment, the attention is focused on the essential point instead of being allowed to lose itself in wonder.

A logical development of this principle leads us to the axiom that a dramatist must never keep a secret from his audience, although this is one of the favorite devices of the novelist. Let us suppose for a moment that the spectators were not let into the secret of Hero's pretty plot, in *Much Ado*, to bring Beatrice and Benedick together. Suppose that, like the heroine and the hero, they were led to believe that each was truly in love with the other. The inevitable revelation of this error would produce a shock of surprise that would utterly scatter their attention; and while they were busy making over their former conception of the situation, they would have no eyes nor ears for what was going on upon the stage. In a novel, the true character of a hypocrite is often hidden until the book is nearly through: then, when the revelation comes, the reader has plenty of time to think back and see how deftly he has been deceived. But in a play, a rogue must be known to be a rogue at his first entrance. The other characters in the play may be kept in the dark until the last act, but the audience must know the secret all the time. In fact, any situation which shows a character suffering from a lack of such knowledge as the audience holds secure always produces a telling effect upon the stage. The spectators are aware of Iago's villainy and know of Desdemona's innocence. The play would not be nearly so strong if, like Othello, they were kept ignorant of the truth.

In order to economise attention, the dramatist

must centre his interest in a few vividly drawn characters and give these a marked preponderance over
the other parts.   Many plays have failed because
of over-elaborateness of detail.   Ben Jonson's comedy of *Every Man in His Humour* would at present
be impossible upon the stage, for the simple reason
that *all* the characters are so carefully drawn that
the audience would not know in whom to be most
interested.   The play is all background and no
foreground.   The dramatist fails to say, " Of all
these sixteen characters, you must listen most attentively to some special two or three "; and, in
consequence, the piece would require a constant
effort of attention that no modern audience would
be willing to bestow.   Whatever may be said about
the disadvantages of the so-called " star system "
in the theatre, the fact remains that the greatest
plays of the world — *Œdipus King, Hamlet, As
You Like It, Tartufe, Cyrano de Bergerac* — have
almost always been what are called " star plays."
The " star system " has an obvious advantage from
the point of view of the dramatist.   When Hamlet enters, the spectators know that they must look
at him; and their attention never wavers to the
minor characters upon the stage.   The play is thus
an easy one to follow: attention is economised and
no effect is lost.

It is a wise plan to use familiar and conventional
types to fill in the minor parts of a play.   The

comic valet, the pretty and witty chambermaid, the *ingénue*, the pathetic old friend of the family, are so well known upon the stage that they spare the mental energy of the spectators and leave them greater vigor of attention to devote to the more original major characters. What is called " comic relief " has a similar value in resting the attention of the audience. After the spectators have been harrowed by Ophelia's madness, they must be diverted by the humor of the grave-diggers in order that their susceptibilities may be made sufficiently fresh for the solemn scene of her funeral.

We have seen that any sudden shock of surprise should be avoided in the theatre, because such a shock must inevitably cause a scattering of attention. It often happens that the strongest scenes of a play require the use of some physical accessory,— a screen in *The School for Scandal*, a horse in *Shenandoah*, a perfumed letter in *Diplomacy*. In all such cases, the spectators must be familiarised beforehand with the accessory object, so that when the climax comes they may devote all of their attention to the action that is accomplished with the object rather than to the object itself. In a quarrel scene, an actor could not suddenly draw a concealed weapon in order to threaten his antagonist. The spectators would stop to ask themselves how he happened to have the weapon by him without their knowing it; and this self-mut-

tered question would deaden the effect of the scene.
The *dénouement* of Ibsen's *Hedda Gabler* requires
that the two chief characters, Eilert Lövborg and
Hedda Tesman, should die of pistol wounds.   The
pistols that are to be used in the catastrophe are
mentioned and shown repeatedly throughout the
early and middle scenes of the play; so that when
the last act comes, the audience thinks not of pistols,
but of murder and suicide.   A striking illustration
of the same dramaturgic principle was shown in
Mrs. Fiske's admirable performance of this play.
The climax of the piece comes at the end of the
penultimate act, when Hedda casts into the fire the
manuscript of the book into which Eilert has put
the great work of his life.   The stove stands ready
at the left of the stage; but when the culminating
moment comes, the spectators must be made to forget the stove in their horror at Hedda's wickedness.
They must, therefore, be made familiar with the
stove in the early part of the act.   Ibsen realised
this, and arranged that Hedda should call for some
wood to be cast upon the fire at the beginning of
the scene.   In acting this incident, Mrs. Fiske
kneeled before the stove in the very attitude that she
was to assume later on when she committed the
manuscript to the flames.   The climax gained
greatly in emphasis because of this device to secure
economy of attention at the crucial moment.

III

In the *Autobiography of Joseph Jefferson*, that humorous and human and instructive book, there is a passage that illustrates admirably the bearing of this same principle of economy of attention upon the actor's art.   In speaking of the joint performances of his half-brother, Charles Burke, and the famous actor-manager, William E. Burton, Jefferson says:

It was a rare treat to see Burton and Burke in the same play: they acted into each other's hands with the most perfect skill; there was no striving to outdo each other. If the scene required that for a time one should be prominent, the other would become the background of the picture, and so strengthen the general effect; by this method they produced a perfectly harmonious work. For instance, Burke would remain in repose, attentively listening while Burton was delivering some humorous speech. This would naturally act as a spell upon the audience, who became by this treatment absorbed in what Burton was saying, and having got the full force of the effect, they would burst forth in laughter or applause; then, by one accord, they became silent, intently listening to Burke's reply, which Burton was now strengthening by the same repose and attention. I have never seen this element in acting carried so far, or accomplished with such admirable results, not even upon the French stage, and I am convinced that the importance of it in reaching the best dramatic effects cannot be too highly estimated. It was this characteristic feature of the acting of these two great artists that always set the audience wondering which was the better. The truth is there was no " better " about the matter. They were not horses running a race, but artists painting a picture; it was not in their

minds which should win, but how they could, by their joint
efforts, produce a perfect work.

I am afraid that this excellent method of team
play is more honored in the breach than in the observance among many of our eminent actors of the
present time. When Richard Mansfield played
the part of Brutus, he destroyed the nice balance of
the quarrel scene with Cassius by attracting all of
the attention of the audience to himself, whereas a
right reading of the scene would demand a constant
shifting of attention from one hero to the other.
When Joseph Haworth spoke the great speech of
Cassius beginning, " Come, Antony, and young
Octavius, come! ", he was shrouded in the shadow
of the tent, while the lime-light fell full upon the
form of Brutus. This arrangement so distracted
the audience from the true dramatic value of the
scene that neither Mansfield's heroic carriage, nor
his eye like Mars to threaten and command, nor
the titanic resonance of his ventriloquial utterance,
could atone for the mischief that was done.

In an earlier paragraph, we noticed the way in
which the " star system " may be used to advantage
by the dramatist to economise the attention of the
audience; but it will be observed, on the other hand,
that the same system is pernicious in its influence
upon the actor. A performer who is accustomed
to the centre of the stage often finds it difficult to
keep himself in the background at moments when

the scene should be dominated by other, and sometimes lesser, actors.   Artistic self-denial is one of
the rarest of virtues.   This is the reason why " all-
star " performances are almost always bad.   A
famous player is cast for a minor part; and in his
effort to exploit his talents, he violates the principle
of economy of attention by attracting undue notice
to a subordinate feature of the performance.
That's villainous, and shows a most pitiful ambition, as Hamlet truly says.   A rare proof of the
genius of the great Coquelin was given by his performances of Père Duval and the Baron Scarpia in
support of the Camille and Tosca of Mme. Sarah
Bernhardt.   These parts are both subordinate;
and, in playing them, Coquelin so far succeeded
in obliterating his own special talents that he never
once distracted the attention of the audience from
the acting of his fellow star.   This was an artistic
triumph worthy of ranking with the same actor's
sweeping and enthralling performance of Cyrano
de Bergerac,— perhaps the richest acting part in
the history of the theatre.

A story is told of how Sir Henry Irving, many
years ago, played the rôle of Joseph Surface at a
special revival of *The School for Scandal* in which
most of the other parts were filled by actors and
actresses of the older generation, who attempted to
recall for one performance the triumphs of their
youth.   Joseph Surface is a hypocrite and a vil-

lain; but the youthful grace of Mr. Irving so charmed a lady in the stalls that she said she " could not bear to see those old unlovely people trying to get the better of that charming young man, Mr. Joseph." Something must have been wrong with the economy of her attention.

The chief reason why mannerisms of walk or gesture or vocal intonation are objectionable in an actor is that they distract the attention of the audience from the effect he is producing to his method of producing that effect. Mansfield's peculiar manner of pumping his voice from his diaphragm and Irving's corresponding system of ejaculating his phrases through his nose gave to the reading of those great artists a rich metallic resonance that was vibrant with effect; but a person hearing either of those actors for the first time was often forced to expend so much of his attention in adjusting his ears to the novel method of voice production that he was unable for many minutes to fix his mind upon the more important business of the play. An actor without mannerisms, like the late Adolf von Sonnenthal, is able to make a more immediate appeal.

IV

At the first night of Mr. E. H. Sothern's *Hamlet*, in the fall of 1900, I had just settled back in my chair to listen to the reading of the soliloquy on suicide, when a woman behind me whispered to her neighbor, " Oh look! There are two fireplaces in the room! " My attention was distracted, and the soliloquy was spoiled; but the fault lay with the stage-manager rather than with the woman who spoke the disconcerting words. If Mr. Sothern was to recite his soliloquy gazing dreamily into a fire in the centre of the room, the stage-manager should have known enough to remove the large fireplace on the right of the stage.

Mme. Sarah Bernhardt, when she acted *Hamlet* in London in 1899, introduced a novel and startling effect in the closet scene between the hero and his mother. On the wall, as usual, hung the counterfeit presentments of two brothers; and when the time came for the ghost of buried Denmark to appear, he was suddenly seen standing luminous in the picture-frame which had contained his portrait. The effect was so unexpected that the audience could look at nothing else, and thus Hamlet and the queen failed to get their proper measure of attention.

These two instances show that the necessity of economising the attention of an audience is just as important to the stage-manager as it is to the dramatist and the actor. In the main, it may be said that any unexpected innovation, any device of stage-management that is by its nature startling, should be avoided in the crucial situations of a

play.   Professor Brander Matthews has given an
interesting illustration of this principle in his essay
on *The Art of the Stage-Manager*, which is included in his volume entitled *Inquiries and Opinions*.
He says:

The stage-manager must ever be on his guard against the
danger of sacrificing the major to the minor, and of letting
some little effect of slight value in itself interfere with the
true interest of the play as a whole.   At the first performance of Mr. Bronson Howard's *Shenandoah,* the opening act of which ends with the firing of the shot on Sumter,
there was a wide window at the back of the set, so that the
spectators could see the curving flight of the bomb and its
final explosion above the doomed fort.   The scenic marvel
had cost time and money to devise; but it was never visible
after the first performance, because it drew attention to
itself, as a mechanical effect, and so took off the minds of
the audience from the Northern lover and the Southern girl,
the Southern lover and the Northern girl, whose loves were
suddenly sundered by the bursting of that fatal shell.   At
the second performance, the spectators did not see the shot,
they only heard the dread report; and they were free to
let their sympathy go forth to the young couples.

Nowadays, perhaps, when the theatre-going public is more used to elaborate mechanism on the stage,
this effect might be attempted without danger.   It
was owing to its novelty at the time that the device
disrupted the attention of the spectators.

But not only novel and startling stage effects
should be avoided in the main dramatic moments
of a play.   Excessive magnificence and elaborateness of setting are just as distracting to the at-

tention as the shock of a new and strange device.
When *The Merchant of Venice* was revived at
Daly's Theatre some years ago, a scenic set of unusual beauty was used for the final act.   The gar-
dens of Portia's palace were shadowy with trees
and dreamy with the dark of evening.   Slowly in
the distance a round and yellow moon rose rolling,
its beams rippling over the moving waters of a
lake.   There was a murmur of approbation in the
audience ; and that murmur was just loud enough to
deaden the lyric beauty of the lines in which Lorenzo and Jessica gave expression to the spirit of
the night.   The audience could not look and listen
at the self-same moment ; and Shakespeare was sacrificed for a lime-light.   A wise stage-manager,
when he uses a set as magnificent, for example, as
the memorable garden scene in Miss Viola Allen's
production of *Twelfth Night*, will raise his curtain on an empty stage, to let the audience enjoy
and even applaud the scenery before the actors
enter.   Then, when the lines are spoken, the spectators are ready and willing to lend them their
ears.

This point suggests a discussion of the advisa-
bility of producing Shakespeare without scenery,
in the very interesting manner that has been employed in recent seasons by Mr. Ben Greet's company of players.   Leaving aside the argument that
with a sceneless stage it is possible to perform all

the incidents of the play in their original order, and thus give the story a greater narrative continuity, it may also be maintained that with a bare stage there are far fewer chances of dispersing the attention of the audience by attracting it to insignificant details of setting.   Certainly, the last act of the *Merchant* would be better without the mechanical moonrise than with it.   But, unfortunately, the same argument for economy of attention works also in the contrary direction.   We have been so long used to scenery in our theatres that a sceneless production requires a new adjustment of our minds to accept the unwonted convention; and it may readily be asserted that this mental adjustment disperses more attention than would be scattered by elaborate stage effects.   At Mr. Greet's first production of *Twelfth Night* in New York without change of scene, many people in the audience could be heard whispering their opinions of the experiment,— a fact which shows that their attention was not fixed entirely upon the play itself. On the whole, it would probably be wisest too produce Shakespeare with very simple scenery, in order, on the one hand, not to dim the imagination of the spectators by elaborate magnificence of setting, and, on the other, not to distract their minds by the unaccustomed conventions of a sceneless stage.

What has been said of scenery may be applied

also to the use of incidental music.   So soon as such music becomes obtrusive, it distracts the attention from the business of the play: and it cannot be insisted on too often that in the theatre the play's the thing.   But a running accompaniment of music, half-heard, half-guessed, that moves to the mood of the play, now swelling to a climax, now softening to a hush, may do much toward keeping the audience in tune with the emotional significance of the action.

A perfect theatrical performance is the rarest of all works of art.   I have seen several perfect statues and perfect pictures; and I have read many perfect poems: but I have never seen a perfect performance in the theatre.   I doubt if such a performance has ever been given, except, perhaps, in ancient Greece.   But it is easy to imagine what its effect would be.   It would rivet the attention throughout upon the essential purport of the play; it would proceed from the beginning to the end without the slightest distraction; and it would convey its message simply and immediately, like the sky at sunrise or the memorable murmur of the sea.

VI

EMPHASIS IN THE DRAMA

By applying the negative principle of economy of attention, the dramatist may, as we have noticed, prevent his auditors at any moment from diverting their attention to the subsidiary features of the scene; but it is necessary for him also to apply the positive principle of emphasis in order to force them to focus their attention on the one most important detail of the matter in hand. The principle of emphasis, which is applied in all the arts, is the principle whereby the artist contrives to throw into vivid relief those features of his work which incorporate the essence of the thing he has to say, while at the same time he gathers and groups within a scarcely noticed background those other features which merely contribute in a minor manner to the central purpose of his plan. This principle is, of course, especially important in the acted drama; and it may therefore be profitable to examine in detail some of the methods which dramatists employ to make their points effectively and bring out the salient features of their plays.

It is obviously easy to emphasise by position.

The last moments in any act are of necessity emphatic because they are the last. During the intermission, the minds of the spectators will naturally dwell upon the scene that has been presented to them most recently. If they think back toward the beginning of the act, they must first think through the concluding dialogue. This lends to curtain-falls a special importance of which our modern dramatists never fail to take advantage.

It is interesting to remember that this simple form of emphasis by position was impossible in the Elizabethan theatre and was quite unknown to Shakespeare. His plays were produced on a platform without a curtain; his actors had to make an exit at the end of every scene; and usually his plays were acted from beginning to end without any intermission. It was therefore impossible for him to bring his acts to an emphatic close by a clever curtain-fall. We have gained this advantage only in recent times because of the improved physical conditions of our theatre.

A few years ago it was customary for dramatists to end every act with a bang that would reverberate in the ears of the audience throughout the *entr'-acte*. Recently our playwrights have shown a tendency toward more quiet curtain-falls. The exquisite close of the first act of *The Admirable Crichton* was merely dreamfully suggestive of the past and future of the action; and the second act ended pictorially, without a word. But whether a curtain-fall gains its effect actively or passively, it should, if possible, sum up the entire dramatic accomplishment of the act that it concludes and foreshadow the subsequent progress of the play.

Likewise, the first moments in an act are of necessity emphatic because they are the first. After an intermission, the audience is prepared to watch with renewed eagerness the resumption of the action. The close of the third act of *Beau Brummel* makes the audience long expectantly for the opening of the fourth; and whatever the dramatist may do after the raising of the curtain will be emphasised because he does it first. An exception must be made of the opening act of a play. A dramatist seldom sets forth anything of vital importance during the first ten minutes of his piece, because the action is likely to be interrupted by late-comers in the audience and other distractions incident to the early hour. But after an intermission, he is surer of attention, and may thrust important matter into the openings of his acts.

The last position, however, is more potent than the first. It is because of their finality that exit speeches are emphatic. It has become customary in the theatre to applaud a prominent actor nearly every time he leaves the stage; and this custom has made it necessary for the dramatist to precede an exit with some speech or action important enough to justify the interruption. Though Shakespeare and his contemporaries knew nothing of the curtain-fall, they at least understood fully the emphasis of exit speeches. They even tagged them with rhyme to give them greater prominence. An actor likes to take advantage of his last chance to move an audience. When he leaves the stage, he wants at least to be remembered.

In general it may be said that any pause in the action emphasises by position the speech or business that immediately preceded it. This is true not only of the long pause at the end of an act: the point is illustrated just as well by an interruption of the play in mid-career, like Mrs. Fiske's ominous and oppressive minute of silence in the last act of *Hedda Gabler*. The employment of pause as an aid to emphasis is of especial importance in the reading of lines.

It is also customary in the drama to emphasise by proportion. More time is given to significant scenes than to dialogues of subsidiary interest. The strongest characters in a play are given most to say and do; and the extent of the lines of the others is proportioned to their importance in the action. Hamlet says more and does more than any other character in the tragedy in which he figures. This is as it should be; but, on the other hand, Polonius, in the same play, seems to receive greater emphasis by proportion than he really deserves. The part is very fully written. Polonius is often on the stage, and talks incessantly whenever he is present; but, after all, he is a man of small importance and fulfils a minor purpose in the plot. He is, therefore, falsely emphasised. That is why the part of Polonius is what French actors call a *faux bon rôle*,— a part that seems better than it is.

In certain special cases, it is advisable to emphasise a character by the ironical expedient of inverse proportion. Tartufe is so emphasised throughout the first two acts of the play that bears his name. Although he is withheld from the stage until the second scene of the third act, so much is said about him that we are made to feel fully his sinister dominance over the household of Orgon; and at his first appearance, we already know him better than we know any of the other characters. In Victor Hugo's *Marion Delorme*, the indomitable will of Cardinal Richelieu is the mainspring of the entire action, and the audience is led to feel that he may at any moment enter upon the stage. But he is withheld until the very final moment of the drama, and even then is merely carried mute across the scene in a sedan-chair. Similarly, in Paul Heyse's *Mary of Magdala*, the supreme person who guides and controls the souls of all the struggling characters is never introduced upon the scene, but is suggested merely through his effect on Mary, Judas, and the other visible figures in the action.

One of the easiest means of emphasis is the use of repetition; and this is a favorite device with Henrik Ibsen. Certain catch-words, which incorporate a recurrent mood of character or situation, are repeated over and over again throughout the course of his dialogue. The result is often similar to that attained by Wagner, in his music-dramas, through the iteration of a *leit-motiv*. Thus in *Rosmersholm*, whenever the action takes a turn that foreshadows the tragic catastrophe, allusion is made to the weird symbol of " white horses." Similarly, in *Hedda Gabler* — to take another instance — the emphasis of repetition is flung on certain leading phrases,— " Fancy that, Hedda! " " Wavy-haired Thea," " Vine-leaves in his hair," and " People don't do such things! "

Another obvious means of emphasis in the drama is the use of antithesis,— an expedient employed in every art. The design of a play is not so much to expound characters as to contrast them. People of varied views and opposing aims come nobly to the grapple in a struggle that vitally concerns them; and the tensity of the struggle will be augmented if the difference between the characters is marked. The comedies of Ben Jonson, which held the stage for two centuries after their author's death, owed their success largely to the fact that they presented a constant contrast of mutually foiling personalities. But the expedient of antithesis is most effectively employed in the balance of scene against scene. What is known as " comic relief " is introduced in various plays, not only, as the phrase suggests, to rest the sensibilities of the audience, but also to emphasise the solemn scenes that come before and after it. It is for this purpose that Shakespeare, in *Macbeth,* introduces a low-comic soliloquy into the midst of a murder scene. Hamlet's ranting over the grave of Ophelia is made more emphatic by antithesis with the foolish banter that precedes it.

This contrast of mood between scene and scene was unknown in ancient plays and in the imitations of them that flourished in the first great period of the French tragic stage. Although the ancient drama frequently violated the three unities of action, time, and place, it always preserved a fourth unity, which we may call unity of mood. It remained for the Spaniards and the Elizabethan English to grasp the dramatic value of the great antithesis between the humorous and the serious, the grotesque and the sublime, and to pass it on through Victor Hugo to the contemporary theatre.

A further means of emphasis is, of course, the use of climax. This principle is at the basis of the familiar method of working up an entrance. My lady's coach is heard clattering behind the scenes. A servant rushes to the window and tells us that his mistress is alighting. There is a ring at the entrance; we hear the sound of footsteps in the hall. At last the door is thrown open, and my lady enters, greeted by a salvo of applause.

A first entrance unannounced is rarely seen upon the modern stage. Shakespeare's *King John* opens very simply. The stage direction reads, "Enter King John, Queen Elinor, Pembroke, Essex, Salisbury and others, with Chatillon"; and then the king speaks the opening line of the play. Yet when Sir Herbert Beerbohm Tree revived this drama at Her Majesty's Theatre in 1899, he devised an elaborate opening to give a climacteric effect to the entrance of the king. The curtain rose upon a vaulted room of state, impressive in its bare magnificence. A throne was set upon a dais to the left, and several noblemen in splendid costumes were lingering about the room. At the back was a Norman corridor approached by a flight of lofty steps which led upward from the level of the stage. There was a peal of trumpets from without, and soon to a stately music the royal guards marched upon the scene. They were followed by ladies with gorgeous dresses sweeping away in long trains borne by pretty pages, and great lords walking with dignity to the music of the regal measure. At last Mr. Tree appeared and stood for a moment at the top of the steps, every inch a king.

Then he strode majestically to the dais, ascended to the throne, and turning about with measured majesty spoke the first line of the play, some minutes after the raising of the curtain.

But not only in the details of a drama is the use of climax necessary. The whole action should sweep upward in intensity until the highest point is reached. In the Shakespearean drama the highest point came somewhat early in the piece, usually in the third act of the five that Shakespeare wrote; but in contemporary plays the climax is almost always placed at the end of the penultimate act,— the fourth act if there are five, and the third act if there are four. Nowadays the four-act form with a strong climax at the end of the third act seems to be most often used. This is the form, for instance, of Ibsen's *Hedda Gabler*, of Mr. Jones's *Mrs. Dane's Defense*, and of Sir Arthur Pinero's *The Second Mrs. Tanqueray*, *The Notorious Mrs. Ebbsmith*, and *The Gay Lord Quex*. Each begins with an act of exposition, followed by an act of rising interest. Then the whole action of the play rushes upward toward the curtain-fall of the third act, after which an act is used to bring the play to a terrible or a happy conclusion.

A less familiar means of emphasis is that which owes its origin to surprise. This expedient must be used with great delicacy, because a sudden and startling shock of surprise is likely to diseconomise the attention of the spectators and flurry them out of a sane conception of the scene. But if a moment of surprise has been carefully led up to by anticipatory suggestion, it may be used to throw into sharp and sudden relief an important point in the play. No one knows that Cyrano de Bergerac is on the stage until he rises in the midst of the crowd in the Hôtel de Bourgogne and shakes his cane at Montfleury. When Sir Herbert Tree played D'Artagnan in *The Musketeers*, he emerged suddenly in the midst of a scene from a suit of old armor standing monumental at the back of the stage,— a *deus ex machinâ* to dominate the situation. American playgoers will remember the disguise of Sherlock Holmes in the last act of Mr. Gillette's admirable melodrama. The appearance of the ghost in the closet scene of *Hamlet* is made emphatic by its unexpectedness.

But perhaps the most effective form of emphasis in the drama is emphasis by suspense. Wilkie Collins, who with all his faults as a critic of life remains the most skilful maker of plots in English fiction, used to say that the secret of holding the attention of one's readers lay in the ability to do three things: " Make 'em laugh; make 'em weep; make 'em wait." There is no use in making an audience wait, however, unless you first give them an inkling of what they are waiting for.

The dramatist must play with his spectators as we play with a kitten when we trail a ball of yarn before its eyes, only to snatch it away just as the kitten leaps for it.

This method of emphasising by suspense gives force to what are known technically as the *scènes à faire* of a drama. A *scène à faire* — the phrase was devised by Francisque Sarcey — is a scene late in a play that is demanded absolutely by the previous progress of the plot. The audience knows that the scene must come sooner or later, and if the element of suspense be ably managed, is made to long for it some time before it comes. In *Hamlet*, for instance, the killing of the king by the hero is of course a *scène à faire*. The audience knows before the first act is over that such a scene is surely coming. When the king is caught praying in his closet and Hamlet stands over him with naked sword, the spectators think at last that the *scène à faire* has arrived; but Shakespeare " makes 'em wait " for two acts more, until the very ending of the play.

In comedy the commonest *scènes à faire* are love scenes that the audience anticipates and longs to see. Perhaps the young folks are frequently on the stage, but the desired scene is prevented by the presence of other characters. Only after many movements are the lovers left alone; and when at

last the pretty moment comes, the audience glows
with long-awaited enjoyment.

It is always dangerous for a dramatist to omit
a *scène à faire*,— to raise in the minds of his audience an expectation that is never satisfied. Sheridan did this in *The School for Scandal* when he
failed to introduce a love scene between Charles
and Maria, and Mr. Jones did it in *Whitewashing
Julia* when he made the audience expect throughout the play a revelation of the truth about the
puff-box and then left them disappointed in the
end. But these cases are exceptional. In general it may be said that an unsatisfied suspense is no
suspense at all.

One of the most effective instances of suspense
in the modern drama is offered in the opening of
John Gabriel Borkman, one of Ibsen's later plays.
Many years before the drama opens, the hero has
been sent to jail for misusing the funds of a bank
of which he was director. After five years of im-
prisonment, he has been released, eight years before
the opening of the play. During these eight years,
he has lived alone in the great gallery of his house,
never going forth even in the dark of night, and
seeing only two people who come to call upon him.
One of these, a young girl, sometimes plays for
him on the piano while he paces moodily up and
down the gallery. These facts are expounded to

the audience in a dialogue between Mrs. Borkman
and her sister that takes place in a lower room below Borkman's quarters; and all the while, in the
pauses of the conversation, the hero is heard walking overhead, pacing incessantly up and down.   As
the act advances, the audience expects at any moment that the hero will appear.   The front door
is thrown open; two minor characters enter; and
still Borkman is heard walking up and down.
There is more talk about him on the stage; the
act is far advanced, and soon it seems that he must
show himself.   From the upper room is heard the
music of the Dance of Death that his young girl
friend is playing for him.   Now to the dismal
measures of the dance the dialogue on the stage
swells to a climax.   Borkman is still heard pacing
in the gallery.   And the curtain falls.   Ten minutes later the raising of the curtain discloses John
Gabriel Borkman standing with his hands behind
his back, looking at the girl who has been playing
for him.   The moment is trebly emphatic,— by
position at the opening of an act, by surprise,
and most of all by suspense.   When the hero is at
last discovered, the audience looks at him.

Of course there are many minor means of emphasis in the theatre, but most of these are artificial
and mechanical.   The proverbial lime-light is one
of the most effective.   The intensity of the dream
scene in Sir Henry Irving's performance of *The*

Bells was due largely to the way in which the single figure of Mathias was silhouetted by a ray of light against a shadowy and inscrutable background ominous with voices.

In this materialistic age, actors even resort to blandishments of costume to give their parts a special emphasis. Our leading ladies are more richly clad than the minor members of their companies. Even the great Mansfield resorted in his performance of Brutus to the indefensible expedient of changing his costume act by act and dressing always in exquisite and subtle colors, while the other Romans, Cassius included, wore the same togas of unaffected white throughout the play. This was a fault in emphasis.

A novel and interesting device of emphasis in stage-direction was introduced by Mr. Forbes-Robertson in his production of *The Passing of the Third Floor Back*. This dramatic parable by Mr. Jerome K. Jerome deals with the moral regeneration of eleven people, who are living in a Bloomsbury boarding-house, through the personal influence of a Passer-by, who is the Spirit of Love incarnate; and this effect is accomplished in a succession of dialogues, in which the Stranger talks at length with one boarder after another. It is necessary, for reasons of reality, that in each of the dialogues the Passer-by and his interlocutor should be seated at their ease. It is also necessary, for reasons of effectiveness in presentation, that the faces of both parties to the conversation should be kept clearly visible to the audience. In actual life, the two people would most naturally sit before a fire; but if a fireplace should be set in either the right or the left wall of the stage and two actors should be seated in front of it, the face of one of them would be obscured from the audience. The producer therefore adopted the expedient of imagining a fireplace in the fourth wall of the room,— the wall that is supposed to stretch across the stage at the line of the footlights. A red-glow from the central lamps of the string of footlights was cast up over a brass railing such as usually bounds a hearth, and behind this, far forward in the direct centre of the stage, two chairs were drawn up for the use of the actors. The right wall showed a window opening on the street, the rear wall a door opening on an entrance hall, and the left wall a door opening on a room adjacent; and in none of these could the fireplace have been logically set. The unusual device of stage-direction, therefore, contributed to the verisimilitude of the set as well as to the convenience of the action. The experiment was successful for the purposes of this particular piece; it did not seem to disrupt the attention of the audience; and the question, therefore, is suggested whether it might not, in many other plays, be advantageous to make imaginary use of the invisible fourth wall.

VII

THE FOUR LEADING TYPES OF DRAMA

I. TRAGEDY AND MELODRAMA

TRAGEDY and melodrama are alike in this,— that each exhibits a set of characters struggling vainly to avert a predetermined doom; but in this essential point they differ,— that whereas the characters in melodrama are drifted to disaster in spite of themselves, the characters in tragedy go down to destruction because of themselves. In tragedy the characters determine and control the plot; in melodrama the plot determines and controls the characters. The writer of melodrama initially imagines a stirring train of incidents, interesting and exciting in themselves, and afterward invents such characters as will readily accept the destiny that he has foreordained for them. The writer of tragedy, on the other hand, initially imagines certain characters inherently predestined to destruction because of what they are, and afterward invents such incidents as will reasonably result from what is wrong within them.

It must be recognised at once that each of these

is a legitimate method for planning a serious play, and that by following either the one or the other, it is possible to make a truthful representation of life. For the ruinous events of life itself divide themselves into two classes — the melodramatic and the tragic — according as the element of chance or the element of character shows the upper hand in them. It would be melodramatic for a man to slip by accident into the Whirlpool Rapids and be drowned; but the drowning of Captain Webb in that tossing torrent was tragic, because his ambition for preëminence as a swimmer bore evermore within itself the latent possibility of his failing in an uttermost stupendous effort.

As Stevenson has said, in his *Gossip on Romance*, "The pleasure that we take in life is of two sorts,— the active and the passive. Now we are conscious of a great command over our destiny; anon we are lifted up by circumstance, as by a breaking wave, and dashed we know not how into the future." A good deal of what happens to us is brought upon us by the fact of what we are; the rest is drifted to us, uninvited, undeserved, upon the tides of chance. When disasters overwhelm us, the fault is sometimes in ourselves, but at other times is merely in our stars. Because so much of life is casual rather than causal, the theatre (whose purpose is to represent life truly) must always rely on melodrama as the most natural and effective type of art for exhibiting some of its most interesting phases. There is therefore no logical reason whatsoever that melodrama should be held in disrepute, even by the most fastidious of critics.

But, on the other hand, it is evident that tragedy is inherently a higher type of art. The melodramatist exhibits merely what may happen; the tragedist exhibits what must happen. All that we ask of the author of melodrama is a momentary plausibility. Provided that his plot be not impossible, no limits are imposed on his invention of mere incident: even his characters will not give him pause, since they themselves have been fashioned to fit the action. But of the author of tragedy we demand an unquestionable inevitability: nothing may happen in his play which is not a logical result of the nature of his characters. Of the melodramatist we require merely the negative virtue that he shall not lie: of the tragedist we require the positive virtue that he shall reveal some phase of the absolute, eternal Truth.

The vast difference between merely saying something that is true and really saying something that gives a glimpse of the august and all-controlling Truth may be suggested by a verbal illustration. Suppose that, upon an evening which at sunset has been threatened with a storm, I observe the sky at midnight to be cloudless, and say, " The stars are

shining still." Assuredly I shall be telling something that is true; but I shall not be giving in any
way a revelation of the absolute. Consider now
the aspect of this very same remark, as it occurs in
the fourth act of John Webster's tragedy, *The
Duchess of Malfi.* The Duchess, overwhelmed with
despair, is talking to Bosola:

Duchess.   I'll go pray; —
      No, I'll go curse.
Bosola   O, fie!
Duchess.   I could curse the stars.
Bosola. O, fearful.
Duchess. And those three smiling seasons of the year
      Into a Russian winter: nay, the world
      To its first chaos.
Bosola.   Look you, the stars shine still.

This brief sentence, which in the former instance
was comparatively meaningless, here suddenly
flashes on the awed imagination a vista of irrevoca-
ble law.

A similar difference exists between the august
Truth of tragedy and the less revelatory truthfulness of melodrama. To understand and to expound the laws of life is a loftier task than merely
to avoid misrepresenting them. For this reason,
though melodrama has always abounded, true tragedy has always been extremely rare. Nearly all
the tragic plays in the history of the theatre have
descended at certain moments into melodrama.
Shakespeare's final version of *Hamlet* stands nearly

on the highest level; but here and there it still exhibits traces of that preëxistent melodrama of the school of Thomas Kyd from which it was derived. Sophocles is truly tragic, because he affords a revelation of the absolute; but Euripides is for the most part melodramatic, because he contents himself with imagining and projecting the merely possible. In our own age, Ibsen is the only author who, consistently, from play to play, commands catastrophes which are not only plausible but unavoidable. It is not strange, however, that the entire history of the drama should disclose very few masters of the tragic; for to envisage the inevitable is to look within the very mind of God.

II. COMEDY AND FARCE

If we turn our attention to the merry-mooded drama, we shall discern a similar distinction between comedy and farce. A comedy is a humorous play in which the actors dominate the action; a farce is a humorous play in which the action dominates the actors. Pure comedy is the rarest of all types of drama; because characters strong enough to determine and control a humorous plot almost always insist on fighting out their struggle to a serious issue, and thereby lift the action above the comic level. On the other hand, unless the characters thus stiffen in their purposes, they usually allow the play to lapse to farce. Pure comedies, however, have now and then been fashioned, without admixture either of farce or of serious drama; and of these *Le Misanthrope* of Molière may be taken as a standard example. The work of the same master also affords many examples of pure farce, which never rises into comedy,— for instance, *Le Medecin Malgré Lui*. Shakespeare nearly always associated the two types within the compass of a single humorous play, using comedy for his major plot and farce for his subsidiary incidents. Farce is decidedly the most irresponsible of all the types of drama. The plot exists for its own sake, and the dramatist need fulfil only two requirements in devising it: — first, he must be funny, and second, he must persuade his audience to accept his situations at least for the moment while they are being enacted. Beyond this latter requisite, he suffers no subservience to plausibility. Since he needs to be believed only for the moment, he is not obliged to limit himself to possibilities. But to compose a true comedy is a very serious task; for in comedy the action must be not only possible and plausible, but must be a necessary result of the nature of the characters. This is the reason why *The School for Scandal* is a greater accomplishment than *The Rivals*, though the latter play is fully as funny as the former. The one is comedy, and the other merely farce.

VIII

THE MODERN SOCIAL DRAMA

THE modern social drama — or the problem play, as it is popularly called — did not come into existence till the fourth decade of the nineteenth century; but in less than eighty years it has shown itself to be the fittest expression in dramaturgic terms of the spirit of the present age; and it is therefore being written, to the exclusion of almost every other type, by nearly all the contemporary dramatists of international importance. This type of drama, currently prevailing, is being continually impugned by a certain set of critics, and by another set continually defended. In especial, the morality of the modern social drama has been a theme for bitter conflict; and critics have been so busy calling Ibsen a corrupter of the mind or a great ethical teacher that they have not found leisure to consider the more general and less contentious questions of what the modern social drama really is, and of precisely on what ground its morality should be determined. It may be profitable, therefore, to stand aloof from such discussion for a moment, in order to inquire calmly what it is all about.

I

Although the modern social drama is sometimes
comic in its mood — *The Gay Lord Quex*, for instance — its main development has been upon the
serious side; and it may be criticised most clearly
as a modern type of tragedy.   In order, therefore,
to understand its essential qualities, we must first
consider somewhat carefully the nature of tragedy
in general.   The theme of all drama is, of course,
a struggle of human wills; and the special theme
of tragic drama is a struggle necessarily foredoomed to failure because the individual human
will is pitted against opposing forces stronger than
itself.   Tragedy presents the spectacle of a human
being shattering himself against insuperable ob-
stacles.   Thereby it awakens pity, because the
hero cannot win, and terror, because the forces
arrayed against him cannot lose.

If we rapidly review the history of tragedy, we
shall see that three types, and only three, have thus
far been devised; and these types are to be distinguished according to the nature of the forces set
in opposition to the wills of the characters.   In
other words, the dramatic imagination of all humanity has thus far been able to conceive only
three types of struggle which are necessarily foredoomed to failure,— only three different varieties
of forces so strong as to defeat inevitably any in-

dividual human being who comes into conflict with
them.   The first of these types was discovered by
Æschylus and perfected by Sophocles; the second
was discovered by Christopher Marlowe and perfected by Shakespeare; and the third was discovered by Victor Hugo and perfected by Ibsen.

The first type, which is represented by Greek
tragedy, displays the individual in conflict with
Fate, an inscrutable power dominating alike the
actions of men and of gods.   It is the God of the
gods,— the destiny of which they are the instru-
ments   and   ministers.   Through   irreverence,
through vainglory, through disobedience, through
weakness, the tragic hero becomes entangled in the
meshes that Fate sets for the unwary; he struggles
and struggles to get free, but his efforts are necessarily of no avail.   He has transgressed the law
of laws, and he is therefore doomed to inevitable
agony.   Because of this superhuman aspect of the
tragic struggle, the Greek drama was religious in
tone, and stimulated in the spectator the reverent
and lofty mood of awe.

The second type of tragedy, which is represented
by the great Elizabethan drama, displays the individual foredoomed to failure, no longer because
of the preponderant power of destiny, but because
of certain defects inherent in his own nature.
The Fate of the Greeks has become humanised
and made subjective.   Christopher Marlowe was

the first of the world's dramatists thus to set the God of all the gods within the soul itself of the man who suffers and contends and dies. But he imagined only one phase of the new and epoch-making tragic theme that he discovered. The one thing that he accomplished was to depict the ruin of an heroic nature through an insatiable ambition for supremacy, doomed by its own vastitude to defeat itself,— supremacy of conquest and dominion with Tamburlaine, supremacy of knowledge with Dr. Faustus, supremacy of wealth with Barabas, the Jew of Malta. Shakespeare, with his wider mind, presented many other phases of this new type of tragic theme. Macbeth is destroyed by vaulting ambition that o'erleaps itself; Hamlet is ruined by irresoluteness and contemplative procrastination. If Othello were not overtrustful, if Lear were not decadent in senility, they would not be doomed to die in the conflict that confronts them. They fall self-ruined, self-destroyed. This second type of tragedy is less lofty and religious than the first; but it is more human, and therefore, to the spectator, more poignant. We learn more about God by watching the annihilation of an individual by Fate; but we learn more about Man by watching the annihilation of an individual by himself. Greek tragedy sends our souls through the invisible; but Elizabethan tragedy answers, " Thou thyself art Heaven and Hell."

The third type of tragedy is represented by the modern social drama. In this the individual is displayed in conflict with his environment; and the drama deals with the mighty war between personal character and social conditions. The Greek hero struggles with the superhuman; the Elizabethan hero struggles with himself; the modern hero struggles with the world. Dr. Stockmann, in Ibsen's *An Enemy of the People*, is perhaps the most definitive example of the type, although the play in which he appears is not, strictly speaking, a tragedy. He says that he is the strongest man on earth because he stands most alone. On the one side are the legions of society; on the other side a man. This is such stuff as modern plays are made of.

Thus, whereas the Greeks religiously ascribed the source of all inevitable doom to divine foreordination, and the Elizabethans poetically ascribed it to the weaknesses the human soul is heir to, the moderns prefer to ascribe it scientifically to the dissidence between the individual and his social environment. With the Greeks the catastrophe of man was decreed by Fate; with the Elizabethans it was decreed by his own soul; with us it is decreed by Mrs. Grundy. Heaven and Hell were once enthroned high above Olympus; then, as with Marlowe's Mephistophilis, they were seated deep in every individual soul; now at last they have been

located in the prim parlor of the conventional dame
next door. Obviously the modern type of tragedy is inherently less religious than the Greek,
since science has as yet induced no dwelling-place
for God. It is also inherently less poetic than the
Elizabethan, since sociological discussion demands
the mood of prose.

II

Such being in general the theme and the aspect
of the modern social drama, we may next consider
briefly how it came into being. Like a great deal
else in contemporary art, it could not possibly
have been engendered before that tumultuous up-
heaval of human thought which produced in history the French Revolution and in literature the
resurgence of romance. During the eighteenth
century, both in England and in France, society
was considered paramount and the individual sub-
servient. Each man was believed to exist for the
sake of the social mechanism of which he formed
a part: the chain was the thing,— not its weakest,
nor even its strongest, link. But the French Revolution and the cognate romantic revival in the arts
unsettled this conservative belief, and made men
wonder whether society, after all, did not exist
solely for the sake of the individual. Early eighteenth century literature is a polite and polished
exaltation of society, and preaches that the ma-

jority is always right; early nineteenth century literature is a clamorous pæan of individualism, and preaches that the majority is always wrong. Considering the modern social drama as a phase of history, we see at once that it is based upon the struggle between these two beliefs. It exhibits always a conflict between the individual revolutionist and the communal conservatives, and expresses the growing tendency of these opposing forces to adjust themselves to equilibrium.

Thus considered, the modern social drama is seen to be inherently and necessarily the product and the expression of the nineteenth century. Through no other type of drama could the present age reveal itself so fully; for the relation between the one and the many, in politics, in religion, in the daily round of life itself, has been, and still remains, the most important topic of our times. The paramount human problem of the last hundred years has been the great, as yet unanswered, question whether the strongest man on earth is he who stands most alone or he who subserves the greatest good of the greatest number. Upon the struggle implicit in this question the modern drama necessarily is based, since the dramatist, in any period when the theatre is really alive, is obliged to tell the people in the audience what they have themselves been thinking. Those critics, therefore, have no ground to stand on who belittle the im-

portance of the modern social drama and regard
it as an arbitrary phase of art devised, for business reasons merely, by a handful of clever playwrights.

Although the third and modern type of tragedy
has grown to be almost exclusively the property of
realistic writers, it is interesting to recall that it
was first introduced into the theatre of the world
by the king of the romantics. It was Victor
Hugo's *Hernani*, produced in 1830, which first exhibited a dramatic struggle between an individual
and society at large. The hero is a bandit and an
outlaw, and he is doomed to failure because of the
superior power of organised society arrayed against
him. So many minor victories were won at that
famous *première* of *Hernani* that even Hugo's fol-
lowers were too excited to perceive that he had
given the drama a new subject and the theatre a
new theme; but this epoch-making fact may now
be clearly recognised in retrospect. *Hernani*, and
all of Victor Hugo's subsequent dramas, dealt,
however, with distant times and lands; and it was
left to another great romantic, Alexander Dumas
père, to be the first to give the modern theme a
modern setting. In his best play, *Antony*, which
exhibits the struggle of a bastard to establish himself in the so-called best society, Dumas brought
the discussion home to his own country and his own
period. In the hands of that extremely gifted

dramatist, Emile Augier, the new type of serious
drama passed over into the possession of the realists, and so downward to the latter-day realistic
dramatists of France and England, Germany and
Scandinavia. The supreme and the most typical
creative figure of the entire period is, of course,
the Norwegian Henrik· Ibsen, who — such is the
irony of progress — despised the romantics of
1830, and frequently expressed a bitter scorn for
those predecessors who discovered and developed
the type of tragedy which he perfected.

III

We are now prepared to inquire more closely
into the specific sort of subject which the modern
social drama imposes on the dramatist. The existence of any struggle between an individual and
the conventions of society presupposes that the individual is unconventional. If the hero were in accord with society, there would be no conflict of
contending forces: he must therefore be one of society's outlaws, or else there can be no play. In
modern times, therefore, the serious drama has been
forced to select as its leading figures men and
women outcast and condemned by conventional society. It has dealt with courtesans (*La Dame Aux
Camélias*), demi-mondaines (*Le Demi-Monde*), erring wives (*Frou-Frou*), women with a past (*The
Second Mrs. Tanqueray*), free lovers (*The No-*

torious Mrs. Ebbsmith), bastards (*Antony; Le Fils Naturel*), ex-convicts (*John Gabriel Borkman*), people with ideas in advance of their time (*Ghosts*), and a host of other characters that are usually considered dangerous to society. In order that the dramatic struggle might be tense, the dramatists have been forced to strengthen the cases of their characters so as to suggest that, perhaps, in the special situations cited, the outcasts were right and society was wrong.   Of course it would be impossible to base a play upon the thesis that, in a given conflict between the individual and society, society was indisputably right and the individual indubitably wrong; because the essential element of struggle would be absent.   Our modern dramatists, therefore, have been forced to deal with *exceptional* outcasts of society,— outcasts with whom the audience might justly sympathise in their conflict with convention.   The task of finding such justifiable outcasts has of necessity narrowed the subject-matter of the modern drama.   It would be hard, for instance, to make out a good case against society for the robber, the murderer, the anarchist. But it is comparatively easy to make out a good case for a man and a woman involved in some sexual relation which brings upon them the censure of society but which seems in itself its own excuse for being.   Our modern serious dramatists have been driven, therefore, in the great majority of cases,

to deal almost exclusively with problems of sex.
This necessity has pushed them upon dangerous
ground. Man is, after all, a social animal. The
necessity of maintaining the solidarity of the family — a necessity (as the late John Fiske luminously
pointed out) due to the long period of infancy in
man — has forced mankind to adopt certain social
laws to regulate the interrelations of men and
women. Any strong attempt to subvert these laws
is dangerous not only to that tissue of convention
called society but also to the development of the
human race. And here we find our dramatists
forced — first by the spirit of the times, which gives
them their theme, and second by the nature of the
dramatic art, which demands a special treatment of
that theme — to hold a brief for certain men and
women who have shuffled off the coil of those very
social laws that man has devised, with his best
wisdom, for the preservation of his race. And the
question naturally follows: Is a drama that does
this moral or immoral?

But the philosophical basis for this question is
usually not understood at all by those critics who
presume to answer the question off-hand in a
spasm of polemics. It is interesting, as an evidence of the shallowness of most contemporary
dramatic criticism, to read over, in the course of
Mr. Shaw's nimble essay on *The Quintessence of
Ibsenism*, the collection which the author has made

of the adverse notices of *Ghosts* which appeared in the London newspapers on the occasion of the first performance of the play in England. Unanimously they commit the fallacy of condemning the piece as immoral because of the subject that it deals with. And, on the other hand, it must be recognised that most of the critical defenses of the same piece, and of other modern works of similar nature, have been based upon the identical fallacy,— that morality or immorality is a question of subject-matter. But either to condemn or to defend the morality of any work of art because of its material alone is merely a waste of words. There is no such thing, *per se*, as an immoral subject for a play: in the treatment of the subject, and only in the treatment, lies the basis for ethical judgment of the piece. Critics who condemn *Ghosts* because of its subject-matter might as well condemn *Othello* because the hero kills his wife — what a suggestion, look you, to carry into our homes! *Macbeth* is not immoral, though it makes night hideous with murder. The greatest of all Greek dramas, *Œdipus King*, is in itself sufficient proof that morality is a thing apart from subject-matter; and Shelley's *The Cenci* is another case in point. The only way in which a play may be immoral is for it to cloud, in the spectator, the consciousness of those invariable laws of life which say to man " Thou shalt not " or " Thou shalt "; and the one thing needful in order that a drama may be moral is that the author shall maintain throughout the piece a sane and truthful insight into the soundness or unsoundness of the relations between his characters.   He must know when they are right and know when they are wrong, and must make clear to the audience the reasons for his judgments.   He cannot be immoral unless he is untrue.   To make us pity his characters when they are vile or love them when they are noxious, to invent excuses for them in situations where they cannot be excused — in a single word, to lie about his characters — this is for the dramatist the one unpardonable sin.   Consequently, the only sane course for a critic who wishes to maintain the thesis that *Ghosts*, or any other modern play, is immoral, is not to hurl mud at it, but to prove by the sound processes of logic that the play tells lies about life; and the only sane way to defend such a piece is not to prate about the " moral lesson " the critic supposes that it teaches, but to prove logically that it tells the truth.

The same test of truthfulness by which we distinguish good workmanship from bad is the only test by which we may conclusively distinguish immoral art from moral.   Yet many of the controversial critics never calm down sufficiently to apply this test.   Instead of arguing whether or not Ibsen tells the truth about Hedda Gabler, they quarrel with him or defend him for talking about her at

all. It is as if zoölogists who had assembled to
determine the truth or falsity of some scientific
theory concerning the anatomy of a reptile should
waste all their time in contending whether or not the
reptile was unclean.

And even when they do apply the test of truthfulness, many critics are troubled by a grave misconception that leads them into error. They make
the mistake of applying *generally* to life certain
ethical judgments that the dramatist means only to
apply *particularly* to the special people in his play.
The danger of this fallacy cannot be too strongly
emphasised. It is not the business of the dramatist to formulate general laws of conduct; he leaves
that to the social scientist, the ethical philosopher,
the religious preacher. His business is merely to
tell the truth about certain special characters involved in certain special situations. If the characters and the situations be abnormal, the dramatist must recognise that fact in judging them; and
it is not just for the critic to apply to ordinary
people in the ordinary situations of life a judgment
thus conditioned. The question in *La Dame Aux
Camélias* is not whether the class of women which
Marguerite Gautier represents is generally esti-
mable, but whether a particular woman of that class,
set in certain special circumstances, was not worthy
of sympathy. The question in *A Doll's House* is
not whether any woman should forsake her hus-

band and children when she happens to feel like it, but whether a particular woman, Nora, living under special conditions with a certain kind of husband, Torwald, really did deem herself justified in leaving her doll's home, perhaps forever. The ethics of any play should be determined, not externally, but within the limits of the play itself. And yet our modern social dramatists are persistently misjudged. We hear talk of the moral teaching of Ibsen,— as if, instead of being a maker of plays, he had been a maker of golden rules. But Mr. Shaw came nearer to the truth with his famous paradox that the only golden rule in Ibsen's dramas is that there is no golden rule.

It must, however, be admitted that the dramatists themselves are not entirely guiltless of this current critical misconception. Most of them happen to be realists, and in devising their situations they aim to be narrowly natural as well as broadly true. The result is that the circumstances of their plays have an *ordinary* look which makes them seem simple transcripts of everyday life instead of special studies of life under peculiar conditions. Consequently the audience, and even the critic, is tempted to judge life in terms of the play instead of judging the play in terms of life. Thus falsely judged, *The Wild Duck* (to take an emphatic instance) is outrageously immoral, although it must be judged moral by the philosophic critic who questions only whether or not Ibsen told the truth about the particular people involved in its depressing story. The deeper question remains: Was Ibsen justified in writing a play which was true and therefore moral, but which necessarily would have an immoral effect on nine spectators out of every ten, because they would instinctively make a hasty and false generalisation from the exceptional and very particular ethics implicit in the story?

For it must be bravely recognised that any statement of truth which is so framed as to be falsely understood conveys a lie. If the dramatist says quite truly, " This particular leaf is sere and yellow," and if the audience quite falsely understands him to say, " All leaves are sere and yellow," the gigantic lie has illogically been conveyed that the world is ever windy with autumn, that spring is but a lyric dream, and summer an illusion. The modern social drama, even when it is most truthful within its own limits, is by its very nature liable to just this sort of illogical conveyance of a lie. It sets forth a struggle between a radical exception and a conservative rule; and the audience is likely to forget that the exception is merely an exception, and to infer that it is greater than the rule. Such an inference, being untrue, is immoral; and in so far as a dramatist aids and abets it, he must be judged dangerous to the theatre-going public.

Whenever, then, it becomes important to determine whether a new play of the modern social type is moral or immoral, the critic should decide first whether the author tells lies specifically about any of the people in his story, and second, provided that the playwright passes the first test successfully, whether he allures the audience to generalise falsely in regard to life at large from the specific circumstances of his play. These two questions are the only ones that need to be decided. This is the crux of the whole matter. And it has been the purpose of the present chapter merely to establish this one point by historical and philosophic criticism, and thus to clear the ground for subsequent discussion.

OTHER PRINCIPLES OF DRAMATIC CRITICISM

OTHER PRINCIPLES
OF DRAMATIC CRITICISM

I

THE PUBLIC AND THE DRAMATIST

No other artist is so little appreciated by the public that enjoys his work, or is granted so little studious consideration from the critically minded, as the dramatist. Other artists, like the novelist, the painter, the sculptor, or the actor, appeal directly to the public and the critics; nothing stands between their finished work and the minds that contemplate it. A person reading a novel by Mr. Howells, or looking at a statue by Saint-Gaudens or a picture by Mr. Sargent, may see exactly what the artist has done and what he has not, and may appreciate his work accordingly. But when the dramatist has completed his play, he does not deliver it directly to the public; he delivers it only indirectly, through the medial interpretation of many other artists,— the actor, the stage-director, the scene-painter, and still others of whom the public seldom hears. If any of these other and medial

artists fails to convey the message that the dramatist intended, the dramatist will fail of his intention,
though the fault is not his own.   None of the general public, and few of the critics, will discern what
the dramatist had in mind, so completely may his
creative thought be clouded by inadequate interpretation.

The dramatist is obviously at the mercy of his actors.   His most delicate love scene may be spoiled
irrevocably by an actor incapable of profound
emotion daintily expressed; his most imaginative
creation of a hard and cruel character may be rendered unappreciable by an actor of too persuasive
charm.   And, on the other hand, the puppets of a
dramatist with very little gift for characterisation
may sometimes be lifted into life by gifted actors
and produce upon the public a greater impression
than the characters of a better dramatist less skilfully portrayed.   It is, therefore, very difficult to
determine whether the dramatist has imagined more
or less than the particular semblance of humanity
exhibited by the actor on the stage.   Othello, as
portrayed by Signor Novelli, is a man devoid of
dignity and majesty, a creature intensely animal
and nervously impulsive; and if we had never read
the play, or seen other performances of it, we
should probably deny to Shakespeare the credit
due for one of his most grand conceptions.   On
the other hand, when we witness Mr. Warfield's

beautiful and truthful performance of *The Music Master*, we are tempted not to notice that the play itself is faulty in structure, untrue in character, and obnoxiously sentimental in tone.   Because Mr. Warfield, by the sheer power of his histrionic genius, has lifted sentimentality into sentiment and conventional theatricism into living truth, we are tempted to give to Mr. Charles Klein the credit for having written a very good play instead of a very bad one.

Only to a slightly less extent is the dramatist at the mercy of his stage-director.   Mrs. Rida Johnson Young's silly play called *Brown of Harvard* was made worth seeing by the genius of Mr. Henry Miller as a producer.   By sheer visual imagination in the setting and the handling of the stage, especially in the first act and the last, Mr. Miller contrived to endow the author's shallow fabric with the semblance of reality.   On the other hand, Mr. Richard Walton Tully's play, *The Rose of the Rancho*, was spoiled by the cleverest stage-director of our day.   Mr. Tully must, originally, have had a story in his mind; but what that story was could not be guessed from witnessing the play.   It was utterly buried under an atmosphere of at least thirty pounds to the square inch, which Mr. Belasco chose to impose upon it.   With the stage-director standing thus, for benefit or hindrance, between the author and the audience, how is the public to appreciate what the dramatist himself has, or has not, done?

An occasion is remembered in theatric circles when, at the tensest moment in the first-night presentation of a play, the leading actress, entering down a stairway, tripped and fell sprawling. Thus a moment which the dramatist intended to be hushed and breathless with suspense was made overwhelmingly ridiculous. A cat once caused the failure of a play by appearing unexpectedly upon the stage during the most important scene and walking foolishly about. A dramatist who has spent many months devising a melodrama which is dependent for its effect at certain moments on the way in which the stage is lighted may have his play sent suddenly to failure at any of those moments if the stage-electrician turns the lights incongruously high or low. These instances are merely trivial, but they serve to emphasise the point that so much stands between the dramatist and the audience that it is sometimes difficult even for a careful critic to appreciate exactly what the dramatist intended.

And the general public, at least in present-day America, never makes the effort to distinguish the intention of the dramatist from the interpretation it receives from the actors and (to a less extent) the stage-director. The people who support the theatre see and estimate the work of the interpretative artists only; they do not see in itself and estimate for its own sake the work of the creative artist whose imaginings are being represented well or badly.   The public in America goes to see actors; it seldom goes to see a play.   If the average theatre-goer has liked a leading actor in one piece, he will go to see that actor in the next piece in which he is advertised to appear.   But very, very rarely will he go to see a new play by a certain author merely because he has liked the last play by the same author.   Indeed, the chances are that he will not even know that the two plays have been written by the same dramatist.   Bronson Howard once told me that he was very sure that not more than one person in ten out of all the people who had seen *Shenandoah* knew who wrote the play.   And I hardly think that a larger proportion of the people who have seen both Mr. Willard in *The Professor's Love Story* and Miss Barrymore in *Alice-Sit-by-the-Fire* could tell you, if you should ask them, that the former play was written by the author of the latter.   How many people who remember vividly Sir Henry Irving's performance of *The Story of Waterloo* could tell you who wrote the little piece?   If you should ask them who wrote the Sherlock Holmes detective stories, they would answer you at once.   Yet *The Story of Waterloo* was written by the author of those same detective stories.

The general public seldoms knows, and almost

never cares, who wrote a play. What it knows, and what it cares about primarily, is who is acting in it. Shakespearean dramas are the only plays that the public will go to see for the author's sake alone, regardless of the actors. It will go to see a bad performance of a play by Shakespeare, because, after all, it is seeing Shakespeare: it will not go to see a bad performance of a play by Sir Arthur Pinero, merely because, after all, it is seeing Pinero. The extraordinary success of *The Master Builder*, when it was presented in New York by Mme. Nazimova, is an evidence of this. The public that filled the coffers of the Bijou Theatre was paying its money not so much to see a play by the author of *A Doll's House* and *Hedda Gabler* as to see a performance by a clever and tricky actress of alluring personality, who was better advertised and, to the average theatre-goer, better known than Henrik Ibsen.

Since the public at large is much more interested in actors than it is in dramatists, and since the first-night critics of the daily newspapers write necessarily for the public at large, they usually devote most of their attention to criticising actors rather than to criticising dramatists. Hence the general theatre-goer is seldom aided, even by the professional interpreters of theatric art, to arrive at an understanding and appreciation, for its own sake, of that share in the entire artistic production which belongs to the dramatist and the dramatist alone.

For, in present-day America at least, production in the theatre is the dramatist's sole means of publication, his only medium for conveying to the public those truths of life he wishes to express. Very few plays are printed nowadays, and those few are rarely read: seldom, therefore, do they receive as careful critical consideration as even third-class novels. The late Clyde Fitch printed *The Girl with the Green Eyes*. The third act of that play exhibits a very wonderful and searching study of feminine jealousy. But who has bothered to read it, and what accredited book-reviewer has troubled himself to accord it the notice it deserves? It is safe to say that that remarkable third act is remembered only by people who saw it acted in the theatre. Since, therefore, speaking broadly, the dramatist can publish his work only through production, it is only through attending plays and studying what lies beneath the acting and behind the presentation that even the most well-intentioned critic of contemporary drama can discover what our dramatists are driving at.

The great misfortune of this condition of affairs is that the failure of a play as a business proposition cuts off suddenly and finally the dramatist's sole opportunity for publishing his thought, even though the failure may be due to any one of many causes other than incompetence on the part of the dramatist. A very good play may fail because of bad acting or crude production, or merely because it has been brought out at the wrong time of the year or has opened in the wrong sort of city. Sheridan's *Rivals*, as everybody knows, failed when it was first presented. But when once a play has failed at the present day, it is almost impossible for the dramatist to persuade any manager to undertake a second presentation of it. Whether good or bad, the play is killed, and the unfortunate dramatist is silenced until his next play is granted a hearing.

II

DRAMATIC ART AND THE THEATRE BUSINESS

ART makes things which need to be distributed; business distributes things which have been made: and each of the arts is therefore necessarily accompanied by a business, whose special purpose is to distribute the products of that art. Thus, a very necessary relation exists between the painter and the picture-dealer, or between the writer and the publisher of books. In either case, the business man earns his living by exploiting the products of the artist, and the artist earns his living by bringing his goods to the market which has been opened by the industry of the business man. The relation between the two is one of mutual assistance; yet the spheres of their labors are quite distinct, and each must work in accordance with a set of laws which have no immediate bearing upon the activities of the other. The artist must obey the laws of his art, as they are revealed by his own impulses and interpreted by constructive criticism; but of these laws the business man may, without prejudice to his efficiency, be largely ignorant. On

the other hand, the business man must do his work
in accordance with the laws of economics,— a science of which artists ordinarily know very little.
Business is, of necessity, controlled by the great
economic law of supply and demand. Of the practical workings of this law the business man is in
a position to know much more than the artist; and
the latter must always be greatly influenced by the
former in deciding as to what he shall make and
how he shall make it. This influence of the publisher, the dealer, the business manager, is nearly
always beneficial, because it helps·the artist to avoid
a waste of work and to conserve and concentrate
his energies; yet frequently the mind of the maker
desires to escape from it, and there is scarcely an
artist worth his salt who has not at some moments,
with the zest of truant joy, made things which
were not for sale. In nearly all the arts it is possible to secede at will from all allegiance to the
business which is based upon them; and Raphael
may write a century of sonnets, or Dante paint a
picture of an angel, without considering the publisher or picture-dealer. But there is one of the
arts — the art of the drama — which can never
be disassociated from its concomitant business —
the business of the theatre. It is impossible to
imagine a man making anything which might
justly be called a play merely to please himself
and with no thought whatever of pleasing also an

audience of others by presenting it before them
with actors on a stage.   But the mere existence of
a theatre, a company of actors, an audience assembled, necessitates an economic organisation and
presupposes a business manager; and this business
manager, who sets the play before the public and
attracts the public to the play, must necessarily
exert a potent influence over the playwright.   The
only way in which a dramatist may free himself
from this influence is by managing his own company, like Molière, or by conducting his own theatre, like Shakespeare.   Only by assuming himself
the functions of the manager can the dramatist
escape from him.   In all ages, therefore, the
dramatist has been forced to confront two sets of
problems rather than one.   He has been obliged
to study and to follow not only the technical laws
of the dramatic art but also the commercial laws of
the theatre business.   And whereas, in the case of
the other arts, the student may consider the painter
and ignore the picture-dealer, or analyse the mind
of the novelist without analysing that of his publisher, the student of the drama in any age must
always take account of the manager, and cannot
avoid consideration of the economic organisation
of the theatre in that age.   Those who are most
familiar with the dramatic and poetic art of Christopher Marlowe and the histrionic art of Edward
Alleyn are the least likely to underestimate the im-

portant influence which was exerted on the early Elizabethan drama by the illiterate but crafty and enterprising manager of these great artists, Philip Henslowe. Students of the Queen Anne period may read the comedies of Congreve, but they must also read the autobiography of Colley Cibber, the actor-manager of the Theatre Royal. And the critic who considers the drama of to-day must often turn from problems of art to problems of economics, and seek for the root of certain evils not in the technical methods of the dramatists but in the business methods of the managers.

At the present time, for instance, the dramatic art in America is suffering from a very unusual economic condition, which is unsound from the business standpoint, and which is likely, in the long run, to weary and to alienate the more thoughtful class of theatre-goers. This condition may be indicated by the one word,— *over-production*. Some years ago, when the theatre trust was organised, its leaders perceived that the surest way to win a monopoly of the theatre business was to get control of the leading theatre-buildings throughout the country and then refuse to house in them the productions of any independent manager who opposed them. By this procedure on the part of the theatre trust, the few managers who maintained their independence were forced to build theatres in those cities where they wished

their attractions to appear. When, a few years
later, the organised opposition to the original theatre trust grew to such dimensions as to become in
fact a second trust, it could carry on its campaign
only by building a new chain of theatres to house
its productions in those cities whose already exist-
ing theatres were in the hands of the original syn-
dicate. As a result of this warfare between the
two trusts, nearly all the chief cities of the country
are now saddled with more theatre-buildings than
they can naturally and easily support. Two theatres stand side by side in a town whose theatre-
going population warrants only one; and there
are three theatres in a city whose inhabitants desire
only two. In New York itself this condition is
even more exaggerated. Nearly every season some
of the minor producing managers shift their
allegiance from one trust to the other; and since
they seldom seem to know very far in advance just
where they will stand when they may wish to make
their next production in New York, the only way
in which they can assure themselves of a Broadway booking is to build and hold a theatre of their
own. Hence, in the last few years, there has been
an epidemic of theatre building in New York.
And this, it should be carefully observed, has resulted from a false economic condition; for new
theatres have been built, not in order to supply a
natural demand from the theatre-going population,

but in defiance of the limits imposed by that demand.

A theatre-building is a great expense to its owners. It always occupies land in one of the most costly sections of a city; and in New York this consideration is of especial importance. The building itself represents a large investment. These two items alone make it ruinous for the owners to let the building stand idle for any lengthy period. They must keep it open as many weeks as possible throughout the year; and if play after play fails upon its stage, they must still seek other entertainments to attract sufficient money to cover the otherwise dead loss of the rent. Hence there exists at present in America a false demand for plays,— a demand, that is to say, which is occasioned not by the natural need of the theatre-going population but by the frantic need on the part of warring managers to keep their theatres open. It is, of course, impossible to find enough first-class plays to meet this fictitious demand; and the managers are therefore obliged to buy up quantities of second-class plays, which they know to be inferior and which they hardly expect the public to approve, because it will cost them less to present these inferior attractions to a small business than it would cost them to shut down some of their superfluous theatres.

We are thus confronted with the anomalous condition of a business man offering for sale, at the regular price, goods which he knows to be inferior, because he thinks that there are just enough customers available who are sufficiently uncritical not to detect the cheat.   Thereby he hopes to cover the rent of an edifice which he has built, in defiance of sound economic principles, in a community that is not prepared to support it throughout the year. No very deep knowledge of economics is necessary to perceive that this must become, in the long run, a ruinous business policy.   Too many theatres showing too many plays too many months in the year cannot finally make money; and this falsity in the economic situation reacts against the dramatic art itself and against the public's appreciation of that art.   Good work suffers by the constant accompaniment of bad work which is advertised in exactly the same phrases; and the public, which is forced to see five bad plays in order to find one good one, grows weary and loses faith.   The way to improve our dramatic art is to reform the economics of our theatre business.   We should produce fewer plays, and better ones.   We should seek by scientific investigation to determine just how many theatres our cities can support, and how many weeks in the year they may legitimately be expected to support them.   Having thus determined the real demand for plays that comes from the theatre-going population, the managers should then bestir themselves to secure sufficient good plays to satisfy that demand. That, surely, is the limit of sound and legitimate business. The arbitrary creation of a further, false demand, and the feverish grasping at a fictitious supply, are evidences of unsound economic methods, which are certain, in the long run, to fail.

III

THE HAPPY ENDING IN THE THEATRE

THE question whether or not a given play should have a so-called happy ending is one that requires more thorough consideration than is usually accorded to it. It is nearly always discussed from one point of view, and one only,— that of the box-office; but the experience of ages goes to show that it cannot rightly be decided, even as a matter of business expediency, without being considered also from two other points of view,— that of art, and that of human interest. For in the long run, the plays that pay the best are those in which a self-respecting art is employed to satisfy the human longing of the audience.

When we look at the matter from the point of view of art, we notice first of all that in any question of an ending, whether happy or unhappy, art is doomed to satisfy itself and is denied the recourse of an appeal to nature. Life itself presents a continuous sequence of causation, stretching on; and nature abhors an ending as it abhors a vacuum. If experience teaches us anything at all, it teaches us that nothing in life is terminal,

169

nothing is conclusive. Marriage is not an end,
as we presume in books; but rather a beginning.
Not even death is final. We find our graves not
in the ground but in the hearts of our survivors,
and our slightest actions vibrate in ever-widening
circles through incalculable time. Any end, therefore, to a novel or a play, must be in the nature
of an artifice; and an ending must be planned not
in accordance with life, which is lawless and illogical, but in accordance with art, whose soul is harmony. It must be a strictly logical result of all
that has preceded it. Having begun with a certain intention, the true artist must complete his
pattern, in accordance with laws more rigid than
those of life; and he must not disrupt his design
by an illogical intervention of the long arm of
coincidence. Stevenson has stated this point in a
letter to Mr. Sidney Colvin: " Make another end
to it? Ah, yes, but that's not the way I write;
the whole tale is implied; I never use an effect when
I can help it, unless it prepares the effects that are
to follow; that's what a story consists in. To
make another end, that is to make the beginning
all wrong." In this passage the whole question is
considered *merely* from the point of view of art.
It is the only point of view which is valid for the
novelist; for him the question is comparatively simple, and Stevenson's answer, emphatic as it is, may
be accepted as final. But the dramatist has yet

another factor to consider,— the factor of his audience.

The drama is a more popular art than the novel, in the sense that it makes its appeal not to the individual but to the populace. It sets a contest of human wills before a multitude gathered together for the purpose of witnessing the struggle; and it must rely for its interest largely upon the crowd's instinctive sense of partisanship. As Marlowe said, in *Hero and Leander,*—

> When two are stripped, long e'er the course begin,
> We wish that one should lose, the other win.

The audience takes sides with certain characters against certain others; and in most cases it is better pleased if the play ends in a victory for the characters it favors. The question therefore arises whether the dramatist is not justified in cogging the dice of chance and intervening arbitrarily to insure a happy outcome to the action, even though that outcome violate the rigid logic of the art of narrative. This is a very important question; and it must not be answered dogmatically. It is safest, without arguing *ex cathedra*, to accept the answer of the very greatest dramatists. Their practice goes to show that such a violation of the strict logic of art is justifiable in comedy, but is not justifiable in what we may broadly call the serious drama. Molière, for instance, nearly al-

ways gave an arbitrary happy ending to his comedies.   Frequently, in the last act, he introduced
a long lost uncle, who arrived upon the scene just
in time to endow the hero and heroine with a fortune and to say " Bless you, my children!" as
the curtain fell.   Molière evidently took the attitude that since any ending whatsoever must be in
the nature of an artifice, and contrary to the laws
of life, he might as well falsify upon the pleasant
side and send his auditors happy to their homes.
Shakespeare took the same attitude in many comedies, of which *As You Like It* may be chosen as
an illustration.   The sudden reform of Oliver and
the tardy repentance of the usurping duke are
both untrue to life and illogical as art; but Shakespeare decided to throw probability and logic to
the winds in order to close his comedy with a general feeling of good-will.   But this easy answer
to the question cannot be accepted in the case of
the serious drama; for — and this is a point that
is very often missed — in proportion as the
dramatic struggle becomes more vital and momentous, the audience demands more and more that
it shall be fought out fairly, and that even the
characters it favors shall receive no undeserved assistance from the dramatist.   This instinct of the
crowd — the instinct by which its demand for fair-
ness is proportioned to the importance of the struggle — may be studied by any follower of profes-

sional base-ball. The spectators at a ball-game are violently partisan and always want the home team to win. In any unimportant game — if the opposing teams, for instance, have no chance to win the pennant — the crowd is glad of any questionable decision by the umpires that favors the home team. But in any game in which the pennant is at stake, a false or bad decision, even though it be rendered in favor of the home team, will be received with hoots of disapproval. The crowd feels, in such a case, that it cannot fully enjoy the sense of victory unless the victory be fairly won. For the same reason, when any important play which sets out to end unhappily is given a sudden twist which brings about an arbitrary happy ending, the audience is likely to be displeased. And there is yet another reason for this displeasure. An audience may enjoy both farce and comedy without believing them; but it cannot fully enjoy a serious play unless it believes the story. In the serious drama, an ending, to be enjoyable, must be credible; in other words, it must, for the sake of human interest, satisfy the strict logic of art. We arrive, therefore, at the paradox that although, in the final act, the comic dramatist may achieve popularity by renouncing the laws of art, the serious dramatist can achieve popularity only by adhering rigidly to a pattern of artistic truth.

This is a point that is rarely understood by people who look at the general question from the point of view of the box-office; they seldom appreciate the fact that a serious play which logically demands an unhappy ending will make more money if it is planned in accordance with the sternest laws of art than if it is given an arbitrary happy ending in which the audience cannot easily believe. The public wants to be pleased, but it wants even more to be satisfied. In the early eighteenth century both *King Lear* and *Romeo and Juliet* were played with fabricated happy endings; but the history of these plays, before and after, proves that the alteration, considered solely from the business standpoint, was an error. And yet, after all these centuries of experience, our modern managers still remain afraid of serious plays which lead logically to unhappy terminations, and, because of the power of their position, exercise an influence over writers for the stage which is detrimental to art and even contrary to the demands of human interest.

IV

THE BOUNDARIES OF APPROBATION

WHEN Hamlet warned the strolling players against making the judicious grieve, and when he lamented that a certain play had proved caviare to the general, he fixed for the dramatic critic the lower and the upper bound for catholicity of approbation. But between these outer boundaries lie many different precincts of appeal. *The Two Orphans* of Dennery and *The Misanthrope* of Molière aim to interest two different types of audience. To say that *The Two Orphans* is a bad play because its appeal is not so intellectual as that of *The Misanthrope* would be no less a solecism than to say that *The Misanthrope* is a bad play because its appeal is not so emotional as that of *The Two Orphans*. The truth is that both stand within the boundaries of approbation. The one makes a primitive appeal to the emotions, without, however, grieving the judicious; and the other makes a refined appeal to the intelligence, without, however, subtly bewildering the mind of the general spectator.

Since success is to a play the breath of life, it is
175

necessary that the dramatist should please his public; but in admitting this, we must remember that
in a city so vast and varied as New York there are
many different publics, which are willing to be
pleased in many different ways. The dramatist
with a new theme in his head may, before he sets
about the task of building and writing his play,
determine imaginatively the degree of emotional
and intellectual equipment necessary to the sort of
audience best fitted to appreciate that theme.
Thereafter, if he build and write for that audience
and that alone, and if he do his work sufficiently
well, he may be almost certain that his play will
attract the sort of audience he has demanded; for
any good play can create its own public by the
natural process of selecting from the whole vast
theatre-going population the kind of auditors it
needs. That problem of the dramatist to please
his public reduces itself, therefore, to two very
simple phases: first, to choose the sort of public
that he wants to please, and second, to direct his
appeal to the mental make-up of the audience which
he himself has chosen. This task, instead of ham-
pering the dramatist, should serve really to assist
him, because it requires a certain concentration of
purpose and consistency of mood throughout his
work.

This concentration and consistency of purpose
and of mood may be symbolised by the figure of

aiming straight at a predetermined target. In the years when firearms were less perfected than they are at present, it was necessary, in shooting with a rifle, to aim lower than the mark, in order to allow for an upward kick at the discharge; and, on the other hand, it was necessary, in shooting with heavy ordnance, to aim higher than the mark, in order to allow for a parabolic droop of the cannon-ball in transit. Many dramatists, in their endeavor to score a hit, still employ these compromising tricks of marksmanship: some aim lower than the judgment of their auditors, others aim higher than their taste. But, in view of the fact that under present metropolitan conditions the dramatist may pick his own auditors, this aiming below them or above them seems (to quote Sir Thomas Browne) "a vanity out of date and superannuated piece of folly." While granting the dramatist entire liberty to select the level of his mark, the critic may justly demand that he shall aim directly at it, without allowing his hand ever to droop down or flutter upward. That he should not aim below it is self-evident: there can be no possible excuse for making the judicious grieve. But that he should not aim above it is a proposition less likely to be accepted off-hand by the fastidious: Hamlet spoke with a regretful fondness of that particular play which had proved caviare to the general. It is, of course, nobler to shoot over the mark than to shoot under it; but it is nobler still to shoot directly at it. Surely there lies a simple truth beneath this paradox of words: — it is a higher aim to aim straight than to aim too high.

If a play be so constituted as to please its consciously selected auditors, neither grieving their judgment by striking lower than their level of appreciation, nor leaving them unsatisfied by snobbishly feeding them caviare when they have asked for bread, it must be judged a good play for its purpose. The one thing needful is that it shall neither insult their intelligence nor trifle with their taste. In view of the many different theatre-going publics and their various demands, the critic, in order to be just, must be endowed with a sympathetic versatility of approbation. He should take as his motto those judicious sentences with which the Autocrat of the Breakfast-Table prefaced his remarks upon the seashore and the mountains: —" No, I am not going to say which is best. The one where your place is is the best for you."

V

IMITATION AND SUGGESTION IN THE DRAMA

There is an old saying that it takes two to make a bargain or a quarrel; and, similarly, it takes two groups of people to make a play,— those whose minds are active behind the footlights, and those whose minds are active in the auditorium. We go to the theatre to enjoy ourselves, rather than to enjoy the actors or the author; and though we may be deluded into thinking that we are interested mainly by the ideas of the dramatist or the imagined emotions of the people on the stage, we really derive our chief enjoyment from such ideas and emotions of our own as are called into being by the observance of the mimic strife behind the footlights. The only thing in life that is really enjoyable is what takes place within ourselves; it is our own experience, of thought or of emotion, that constitutes for us the only fixed and memorable reality amid the shifting shadows of the years; and the experience of anybody else, either actual or imaginary, touches us as true and permanent only when it calls forth an answering imagination

of our own.   Each of us, in going to the theatre,
carries with him, in his own mind, the real stage
on which the two hours' traffic is to be enacted;
and what passes behind the footlights is efficient
only in so far as it calls into activity that im-
manent potential clash of feelings and ideas within
our brain.   It is the proof of a bad play that it
permits us to regard it with no awakening of mind;
we sit and stare over the footlights with a brain
that remains blank and unpopulated; we do not
create within our souls that real play for which the
actual is only the occasion; and since we remain
empty of imagination, we find it impossible to
enjoy *ourselves*.   Our feeling in regard to a bad
play might be phrased in the familiar sentence,—
" This is all very well; but what is it *to me?* "
The piece leaves us unresponsive and aloof; we
miss that answering and *tallying* of mind — to
use Whitman's word — which is the soul of all experience of worthy art.   But a good play helps us
to enjoy ourselves by making us aware of ourselves; it forces us to think and feel.   We may
think differently from the dramatist, or feel emotions quite dissimilar from those of the imagined
people of the story; but, at any rate, our minds
are consciously aroused, and the period of our at-
tendance at the play becomes for us a period of
real experience.   The only thing, then, that counts
in theatre-going is not what the play can give us,

but what we can give the play. The enjoyment
of the drama is subjective, and the province of the
dramatist is merely to appeal to the subtle sense of
life that is latent in ourselves.

There are, in the main, two ways in which this
appeal may be made effectively. The first is by
imitation of what we have already seen around us;
and the second is by suggestion of what we have
already experienced within us. We have seen people who were like Hedda Gabler; we have been
people who were like Hamlet. The drama of facts
stimulates us like our daily intercourse with the
environing world; the drama of ideas stimulates us
like our mystic midnight hours of solitary musing.
Of the drama of imitation we demand that it shall
remain appreciably within the limits of our own
actual observation; it must deal with our own country and our own time, and must remind us of our
daily inference from the affairs we see busy all
about us. The drama of facts cannot be trans-
planted; it cannot be made in France or Germany
and remade in America; it is localised in place and
time, and has no potency beyond the bounds of its
locality. But the drama of suggestion is unlimited in its possibilities of appeal; ideas are without
date, and burst the bonds of locality and language.
Americans may see the ancient Greek drama of
Œdipus King played in modern French by Mounet-
Sully, and may experience thereby that inner over-

whelming sense of the sublime which is more real than the recognition of any simulated actuality.

The distinction between the two sources of appeal in drama may be made a little more clear by an illustration from the analogous art of literature. When Whitman, in his poem on *Crossing Brooklyn Ferry*, writes, " Crowds of men and women attired in the usual costumes! ", he reminds us of the environment of our daily existence, and may or may not call forth within us some recollection of experience.   In the latter event, his utterance is a failure; in the former, he has succeeded in stimulating activity of mind by the process of setting before us a reminiscence of the actual.   But when, in the *Song of Myself*, he writes, " We found our own, O my Soul, in the calm and cool of the daybreak," he sets before us no imitation of habituated externality, but in a flash reminds us by suggestion of so much, that to recount the full experience thereof would necessitate a volume.   That second sentence may well keep us busy for an evening, alive in recollection of uncounted hours of calm wherein the soul has ascended to recognition of its universe; the first sentence we may dismiss at once, because it does not make anything important happen in our consciousness.

It must be confessed that the majority of the plays now shown in our theatres do not stimulate us to any responsive activity of mind, and therefore do not permit us, in any real sense, to enjoy ourselves. But those that, in a measure, do succeed in this prime endeavor of dramatic art may readily be grouped into two classes, according as their basis of appeal is imitation or suggestion.

VI

HOLDING THE MIRROR UP TO NATURE

DOUBTLESS no one would dissent from Hamlet's dictum that the purpose of playing is " to hold, as 't were, the mirror up to nature "; but this statement is so exceedingly simple that it is rather difficult to understand. What special kind of mirror did that wise dramatic critic have in mind when he coined this memorable phrase? Surely he could not have intended the sort of flat and clear reflector by the aid of which we comb our hair; for a mirror such as this would represent life with such sedulous exactitude that we should gain no advantage from looking at the reflection rather than at the life itself which was reflected. If I wish to see the tobacco jar upon my writing table, I look at the tobacco jar: I do not set a mirror up behind it and look into the mirror. But suppose I had a magic mirror which would reflect that jar in such a way as to show me not only its outside but also the amount of tobacco shut within it. In this latter case, a glance at the represented image would spare me a more laborious examination of the actual object.

Now Hamlet must have had in mind some magic mirror such as this, which, by its manner of reflecting life, would render life more intelligible. Goethe once remarked that the sole excuse for the existence of works of art is that they are different from the works of nature. If the theatre showed us only what we see in life itself, there would be no sense at all in going to the theatre. Assuredly it must show us more than that; and it is an interesting paradox that in order to show us more it has to show us less. The magic mirror must refuse to reflect the irrelevant and non-essential, and must thereby concentrate attention on the pertinent and essential phases of nature. That mirror is the best that reflects the least which does not matter, and, as a consequence, reflects most clearly that which does. In actual life, truth is buried beneath a bewilderment of facts. Most of us seek it vainly, as we might seek a needle in a haystack. In this proverbial search we should derive no assistance from looking at a reflection of the haystack in an ordinary mirror. But imagine a glass so endowed with a selective magic that it would not reflect hay but would reflect steel. Then, assuredly, there would be a valid and practical reason for holding the mirror up to nature.

The only real triumph for an artist is not to show us a haystack, but to make us see the needle buried in it,— not to reflect the trappings and the suits of life, but to suggest a sense of that within which passeth show. To praise a play for its exactitude in representing facts would be a fallacy of criticism. The important question is not how nearly the play reflects the look of life, but how much it helps the audience to understand life's meaning. The sceneless stage of the Elizabethan *As You Like It* revealed more meanings than our modern scenic forests empty of Rosalind and Orlando. There is no virtue in reflection unless there be some magic in the mirror. Certain enterprising modern managers permit their press agents to pat them on the back because they have set, say, a locomotive on the stage; but why should we pay two dollars to see a locomotive in the theatre when we may see a dozen locomotives in the Grand Central Station without paying anything? Why, indeed! — unless the dramatist contrives to reveal an imaginable human mystery throbbing in the palpitant heart — no, not of the locomotive, but of the locomotive-engineer. That is something that we could not see at all in the Grand Central Station, unless we were endowed with eyes as penetrant as those of the dramatist himself.

But not only must the drama render life more comprehensible by discarding the irrelevant, and attracting attention to the essential; it must also render us the service of bringing to a focus that phase of life it represents. The mirror which the

dramatist holds up to nature should be a concave
mirror, which concentrates the rays impinging on
it to a luminous focal image. Hamlet was too
much a metaphysician to busy his mind about the
simpler science of physics; but surely this figure
of the concave mirror, with its phenomenon of concentration, represents most suggestively his belief
concerning the purpose of playing and of plays.
The trouble with most of our dramas is that they
render scattered and incoherent images of life;
they tell us many unimportant things, instead of
telling us one important thing in many ways.
They reveal but little, because they reproduce too
much. But it is only by bringing all life to a
focus in a single luminous idea that it is possible,
in the two hours' traffic of the stage, "to show
virtue her own feature, scorn her own image, and
the very age and body of the time his form and
pressure."

An interesting instance of how a dramatist, by
holding, as it were, a concave mirror up to nature,
may concentrate all life to a focus in a single
luminous idea is afforded by that justly celebrated
drama entitled *El Gran Galeoto*, by Don José
Echegaray. This play was first produced at the
Teatro Español on March 19, 1881, and achieved
a triumph that soon diffused the fame of its author, which till then had been but local, beyond
the Pyrenees. It is now generally recognised as

one of the standard monuments of the modern social drama. It owes its eminence mainly to the unflinching emphasis which it casts upon a single great idea. This idea is suggested in its title.

In the old French romance of Launcelot of the Lake, it was Gallehault who first prevailed on Queen Guinevere to give a kiss to Launcelot: he was thus the means of making actual their potential guilty love. His name thereafter, like that of Pandarus of Troy, became a symbol to designate a go-between, inciting to illicit love. In the fifth canto of the *Inferno*, Francesca da Rimini narrates to Dante how she and Paolo read one day, all unsuspecting, the romance of Launcelot; and after she tells how her lover, allured by the suggestion of the story, kissed her on the mouth all trembling, she adds,

Galeotto fu'l libro e chi lo scrisse,

which may be translated, " The book and the author of it performed for us the service of Gallehault." Now Echegaray, desiring to retell in modern terms the old familiar story of a man and a woman who, at first innocent in their relationship, are allured by unappreciable degrees to the sudden realisation of a great passion for each other, asked himself what force it was, in modern life, which would perform for them most tragically the sinful service of Gallehault. Then it struck him

that the great Gallehault of modern life — *El
Gran Galeoto* — was the impalpable power of gossip, the suggestive force of whispered opinion, the
prurient allurement of evil tongues.   Set all society
to glancing slyly at a man and a woman whose relation to each other is really innocent, start the
wicked tongues a-babbling, and you will stir up
a whirlwind which will blow them giddily into
each other's arms.   Thus the old theme might be
recast for the purposes of modern tragedy.
Echegaray himself, in the critical prose prologue
which he prefixed to his play, comments upon the
fact that the chief character and main motive force
of the entire drama can never appear upon the
stage, except in hints and indirections; because the
great Gallehault of his story is not any particular
person, but rather all slanderous society at large.
As he expresses it, the villain-hero of his drama is
Todo el mundo,— everybody, or all the world.

This, obviously, is a great idea for a modern
social drama, because it concentrates within itself
many of the most important phases of the perennial struggle between the individual and society;
and this great idea is embodied with direct, un-
wavering simplicity in the story of the play.   Don
Julián, a rich merchant about forty years of age,
is ideally married to Teodora, a beautiful woman
in her early twenties, who adores him.   He is a
generous and kindly man; and upon the death of

an old and honored friend, to whose assistance in
the past he owes his present fortune, he adopts
into his household the son of this friend, Ernesto.
Ernesto is twenty-six years old; he reads poems
and writes plays, and is a thoroughly fine fellow.
He feels an almost filial affection for Don Julián
and a wholesome brotherly friendship for Teodora.
They, in turn, are beautifully fond of him. Naturally, he accompanies them everywhere in the
social world of Madrid; he sits in their box at the
opera, acting as Teodora's escort when her husband is detained by business; and he goes walking
with Teodora of an afternoon. Society, with
sinister imagination, begins to look askance at the
triangulated household; tongues begin to wag;
and gossip grows. Tidings of the evil talk about
town are brought to Don Julián by his brother,
Don Severo, who advises that Ernesto had better
be requested to live in quarters of his own. Don
Julián nobly repels this suggestion as insulting;
but Don Severo persists that only by such a course
may the family name be rendered unimpeachable
upon the public tongue.

Ernesto, himself, to still the evil rumors, goes to
live in a studio alone. This simple move on his
part suggests to everybody — *todo el mundo* —
that he must have had a real motive for making it.
Gossip increases, instead of diminishing; and the

emotions of Teodora, Don Julián, and himself are
stirred to the point of nervous tensity. Don
Julián, in spite of his own sweet reasonableness,
begins subtly to wonder if there could be, by any
possibility, any basis for his brother's vehemence.
Don Severo's wife, Doña Mercedes, repeats the
talk of the town to Teodora, and turns her imagination inward, till it falters in self-questionings.
Similarly the great Gallehault,— which is the word
of all the world,— whispers unthinkable and tragic
possibilities to the poetic and self-searching mind
of Ernesto. He resolves to seek release in Argen-
tina. But before he can sail away, he overhears,
in a fashionable café, a remark which casts a slur
on Teodora, and strikes the speaker of the insult
in the face. A duel is forthwith arranged, to take
place in a vacant studio adjacent to Ernesto's.
When Don Julián learns about it, he is troubled by
the idea that another man should be fighting for
his wife, and rushes forthwith to wreak vengeance
himself on the traducer. Teodora hears the news;
and in order to prevent both her husband and
Ernesto from endangering their lives, she rushes
to Ernesto's rooms to urge him to forestall hos-
tilities. Meanwhile her husband encounters the
slanderer, and is severely wounded. He is carried
to Ernesto's studio. Hearing people coming,
Teodora hides herself in Ernesto's bedroom, where

she is discovered by her husband's attendants. Don Julián, wounded and enfevered, now at last believes the worst.

Ernesto seeks and slays Don Julián's assailant. But now the whole world credits what the whole world has been whispering. In vain Ernesto and Teodora protest their innocence to Don Severo and to Doña Mercedes. In vain they plead with the kindly and noble man they both revere and love. Don Julián curses them, and dies believing in their guilt. Then at last, when they find themselves cast forth isolate by the entire world, their common tragic loneliness draws them to each other. They are given to each other by the world. The insidious purpose of the great Gallehault has been accomplished; and Ernesto takes Teodora for his own.

BLANK VERSE ON THE CONTEMPORARY STAGE

I⊤ is amazing how many people seem to think that the subsidiary fact that a certain play is written in verse makes it of necessity dramatic literature. Whether or not a play is literature depends not upon the medium of utterance the characters may use, but on whether or not the play sets forth a truthful view of some momentous theme; and whether or not a play is drama depends not upon its trappings and its suits, but on whether or not it sets forth a tense and vital struggle between individual human wills. *The Second Mrs. Tanqueray* fulfils both of these conditions and is dramatic literature, while the poetic plays of Mr. Stephen Phillips stand upon a lower plane, both as drama and as literature, even though they are written in the most interesting blank verse that has been developed since Tennyson. *Shore Acres*, which was written in New England dialect, was, I think, dramatic literature. Mr. Percy Mackaye's *Jeanne d'Arc*, I think, was not, even though in merely literary merit it revealed many excellent qualities.

Jeanne d'Arc was not a play; it was a narrative in verse, with lyric interludes. It was a thing to be read rather than to be acted. It was a charming poetic story, but it was not an interesting contribution to the stage. Most people felt this, I am sure; but most people lacked the courage of their feeling, and feared to confess that they were wearied by the piece, lest they should be suspected of lack of taste. I believe thoroughly in the possibility of poetic drama at the present day; but it must be drama first and foremost, and poetry only secondarily. Mr. Mackaye, like a great many other aspirants, began at the wrong end: he made his piece poetry first and foremost, and drama only incidentally. And I think that the only way to prepare the public for true poetic drama is to educate the public's faith in its right to be bored in the theatre by poetry that is not dramatic. Performances of *Pippa Passes* and *The Sunken Bell* exert a very unpropitious influence upon the mood of the average theatre-goer. These poems are not plays; and the innocent spectator, being told that they are, is made to believe that poetic drama must be necessarily a soporific thing. And when this belief is once lodged in his uncritical mind, it is difficult to dispel it, even with a long course of *Othello* and *Hamlet*. *Paolo and Francesca* was a good poem, but a bad play; and its weakness as a play was not excusable by its beauty as a poem. *Cyrano de Bergerac* was a good play, first of all, and a good poem also; and even a public that fears to seem Philistine knew the difference instinctively.

Mme. Nazimova has been quoted as saying that she would never act a play in verse, because in speaking verse she could not be natural. But whether an actor may be natural or not depends entirely upon the kind of verse the author has given him to speak. Three kinds of blank verse are known in English literature,— lyric, narrative, and dramatic. By lyric blank verse I mean verse like that of Tennyson's *Tears, Idle Tears;* by narrative, verse like that of Mr. Stephen Phillips's *Marpessa* or Tennyson's *Idylls of the King;* by dramatic, verse like that of the murder scene in *Macbeth.* The Elizabethan playwrights wrote all three kinds of blank verse, because their drama was a platform drama and admitted narrative and lyric as well as dramatic elements. But because of the development in modern times of the physical conditions of the theatre, we have grown to exclude from the drama all non-dramatic elements. Narrative and lyric, for their own sakes, have no place upon the modern stage; they may be introduced only for a definite dramatic purpose. Only one of the three kinds of blank verse that the Elizabethan playwrights used is, therefore, serviceable on the modern stage. But our poets, because of inexperience in the theatre, insist on writing the other two. For this reason, and for this reason only, do modern actors like Mme. Nazimova complain of plays in verse.

Mr. Percy Mackaye's verse in *Jeanne d'Arc*, for example, was at certain moments lyric, at most moments narrative, and scarcely ever dramatic in technical mold and manner. It resembled the verse of Tennyson more nearly than it resembled that of any other master; and Tennyson was a narrative, not a dramatic, poet. It set a value on literary expression for its own sake rather than for the purpose of the play; it was replete with elaborately lovely phrases; and it admitted the inversions customary in verse intended for the printed page. But I am firm in the belief that verse written for the modern theatre should be absolutely simple. It should incorporate no words, however beautiful, that are not used in the daily conversation of the average theatre-goer; it should set these words only in their natural order, and admit no inversions whatever for the sake of the line; and it should set a value on expression, never for its own sake, but solely for the sake of the dramatic purpose to be accomplished in the scene. Verse such as this would permit of every rhythmical variation known in English prosody, and through the appeal of its rhythm would offer the dramatist opportunities for emotional effect that prose would not allow him; but at the same time it could be spoken with entire naturalness by actors as ultra-modern as Mme. Nazimova.

Mr. Stephen Phillips has not learned this lesson, and the verse that he has written in his plays is the same verse that he used in his narratives, *Marpessa* and *Christ in Hades*. It is great narrative blank verse, but for dramatic uses it is too elaborate. Mr. Mackaye has started out on the same mistaken road: in *Jeanne d'Arc* his prosody is that of closet-verse, not theatre-verse. The poetic drama will be doomed to extinction on the modern stage unless our poets learn the lesson of simplicity. I shall append some lines of Shakespeare's to illustrate the ideal of directness toward which our latter-day poetic dramatists should strive. When Lear holds the dead Cordelia in his arms, he says:

> Her voice was ever soft,
> Gentle, and low,— an excellent thing in woman.

Could any actor be unnatural in speaking words so simple, so familiar, and so naturally set? Viola says to Orsino:

> My father had a daughter loved a man,
> As it might be, perhaps, were I woman,
> I should your lordship.

Here again the words are all colloquial and are set in their accustomed order; but by sheer mastery of rhythm the poet contrives to express the tremulous hesitance of Viola's mood as it could not be expressed in prose. There is a need for verse upon the stage, if the verse be simple and colloquial; and there is a need for poetry in the drama, provided that the play remain the thing and the poetry contribute to the play.

VIII

DRAMATIC LITERATURE AND THEATRIC JOURNALISM

ONE reason why journalism is a lesser thing than literature is that it subserves the tyranny of timeliness. It narrates the events of the day and discusses the topics of the hour, for the sole reason that they happen for the moment to float uppermost upon the current of human experience. The flotsam of this current may occasionally have dived up from the depths and may give a glimpse of some underlying secret of the sea; but most often it merely drifts upon the surface, indicative of nothing except which way the wind lies. Whatever topic is the most timely to-day is doomed to be the most untimely to-morrow. Where are the journals of yester-year? Dig them out of dusty files, and all that they say will seem wearisomely old, for the very reason that when it was written it seemed spiritedly new. Whatever wears a date upon its forehead will soon be out of date. The main interest of news is newness; and nothing slips so soon behind the times as novelty.

With timeliness, as an incentive, literature has

absolutely no concern. Its purpose is to reveal what was and is and evermore shall be. It can never grow old, for the reason that it has never attempted to be new. Early in the nineteenth century, the gentle Elia revolted from the tyranny of timeliness. " Hang the present age! ", said he, " I'll write for antiquity." The timely utterances of his contemporaries have passed away with the times that called them forth: his essays live perennially new. In the dateless realm of revelation, antiquity joins hands with futurity. There can be nothing either new or old in any utterance which is really true or beautiful or right.

In considering a given subject, journalism seeks to discover what there is in it that belongs to the moment, and literature seeks to reveal what there is in it that belongs to eternity. To journalism facts are important because they are facts; to literature they are important only in so far as they are representative of recurrent truths. Literature speaks because it has something to say: journalism speaks because the public wants to be talked to. Literature is an emanation from an inward impulse: but the motive of journalism is external; it is fashioned to supply a demand outside itself. It is frequently said, and is sometimes believed, that the province of journalism is to mold public opinion; but a consideration of actual conditions indicates rather that its province is to find out what the opinion of some section of the public is, and then to formulate it and express it. The successful journalist tells his readers what they want to be told. He becomes their prophet by making clear to them what they themselves are thinking. He influences people by agreeing with them. In doing this he may be entirely sincere, for his readers may be right and may demand from him the statement of his own most serious convictions; but the fact remains that his motive for expression is centred in them instead of in himself. It is not thus that literature is motivated. Literature is not a formulation of public opinion, but an expression of personal and particular belief. For this reason it is more likely to be true. Public opinion is seldom so important as private opinion. Socrates was right and Athens wrong. Very frequently the multitude at the foot of the mountain are worshiping a golden calf, while the prophet, lonely and aloof upon the summit, is hearkening to the very voice of God.

The journalist is limited by the necessity of catering to majorities; he can never experience the felicity of Dr. Stockmann, who felt himself the strongest man on earth because he stood most alone. It may sometimes happen that the majority is right; but in that case the agreement of the journalist is an unnecessary utterance. The truth was known before he spoke, and his speak-

ing is superfluous. What is popularly said about
the educative force of journalism is, for the most
part, baseless. Education occurs when a man is
confronted with something true and beautiful and
good which stimulates to active life that " bright
effluence of bright essence increate " which dwells
within him. The real ministers of education must
be, in Emerson's phrase, " lonely, original, and
pure." But journalism is popular instead of
lonely, timely rather than original, and expedient
instead of pure. Even at its best, journalism
remains an enterprise; but literature at its best
becomes no less than a religion.

These considerations are of service in studying
what is written for the theatre. In all periods,
certain contributions to the drama have been journalistic in motive and intention, while certain others
have been literary. There is a good deal of journalism in the comedies of Aristophanes. He often
chooses topics mainly for their timeliness, and
gathers and says what happens to be in the air.
Many of the Elizabethan dramatists, like Dekker
and Heywood and Middleton for example, looked
at life with the journalistic eye. They collected and
disseminated news. They were, in their own time,
much more " up to date " than Shakespeare, who
chose for his material old stories that nearly every
one had read. Ben Jonson's *Bartholomew Fair* is
glorified journalism. It brims over with con-

temporary gossip and timely witticisms. Therefore it is out of date to-day, and is read only by
people who wish to find out certain facts of London life in Jonson's time. *Hamlet* in 1602 was
not a novelty; but it is still read and seen by
people who wish to find out certain truths of life
in general.

At the present day, a very large proportion of
the contributions to the theatre must be classed
and judged as journalism. Such plays, for instance, as *The Lion and the Mouse* and *The Man
of the Hour* are nothing more or less than dramatised newspapers. A piece of this sort, however effective it may be at the moment, must soon
suffer the fate of all things timely and slip behind the times. Whenever an author selects a
subject because he thinks the public wants him
to talk about it, instead of because he knows he
wants to talk about it to the public, his motive
is journalistic rather than literary. A timely
topic may, however, be used to embody a truly
literary intention. In *The Witching Hour*, for
example, journalism was lifted into literature by
the sincerity of Mr. Thomas's conviction that
he had something real and significant to say.
The play became important because there was a
man behind it. Individual personality is perhaps
the most dateless of all phenomena. The fact
of any great individuality once accomplished and

achieved becomes contemporary with the human race and sloughs off the usual limits of past and future.

Whatever Mr. J. M. Barrie writes is literature, because he dwells isolate amidst the world in a wise minority of one. The things that he says are of importance because nobody else could have said them. He has achieved individuality, and thereby passed out of hearing of the ticking of clocks into an ever-ever land where dates are not and consequently epitaphs can never be. What he utters is of interest to the public, because his motive for speaking is private and personal. Instead of telling people what they think that they are thinking, he tells them what they have always known but think they have forgotten. He performs, for this oblivious generation, the service of a great reminder. He lures us from the strident and factitious world of which we read daily in the first pages of the newspapers, back to the serene eternal world of little, nameless, unremembered acts of kindness and of love. He educates the many, not by any crass endeavor to formulate or even to mold the opinion of the public, but by setting simply before them thoughts which do often lie too deep for tears.

The distinguishing trait of Mr. Barrie's genius is that he looks upon life with the simplicity of a child and sees it with the wisdom of a woman.

He has a woman's subtlety of insight, a child's concreteness of imagination. He is endowed (to reverse a famous phrase of Matthew Arnold's) with a sweet unreasonableness. He understands life not with his intellect but with his sensibilities. As a consequence, he is familiar with all the tremulous, delicate intimacies of human nature that every woman knows, but that most men glimpse only in moments of exalted sympathy with some wise woman whom they love. His insight has that absoluteness which is beyond the reach of intellect alone. He knows things for the unutterable woman's reason,—" because . . ."

But with this feminine, intuitive understanding of humanity, Mr. Barrie combines the distinctively masculine trait of being able to communicate the things that his emotions know. The greatest poets would, of course, be women, were it not for the fact that women are in general incapable of revealing through the medium of articulate art the very things they know most deeply. Most of the women who have written have said only the lesser phases of themselves; they have unwittingly withheld their deepest and most poignant wisdom because of a native reticence of speech. Many a time they reach a heaven of understanding shut to men; but when they come back, they cannot tell the world. The rare artists among women, like Sappho and Mrs. Browning and

Christina Rossetti and Laurence Hope, in their several different ways, have gotten themselves expressed only through a sublime and glorious unashamedness. As Hawthorne once remarked very wisely, women have achieved art only when they have stood naked in the market-place. But men in general are not withheld by a similar hesitance from saying what they feel most deeply. No woman could have written Mr. Barrie's biography of his mother; but for a man like him there is a sort of sacredness in revealing emotion so private as to be expressible only in the purest speech. Mr. Barrie was apparently born into the world of men to tell us what our mothers and our wives would have told us if they could,— what in deep moments they have tried to tell us, trembling exquisitely upon the verge of the words. The theme of his best work has always been "what every woman knows." In expressing this, he has added to the permanent recorded knowledge of humanity; and he has thereby lifted his plays above the level of theatric journalism to the level of true dramatic literature.

IX

THE INTENTION OF PERMANENCE

At Coney Island and Atlantic City and many other seaside resorts whither the multitude drifts to drink oblivion of a day, an artist may be watched at work modeling images in the sand. These he fashions deftly, to entice the immediate pennies of the crowd; but when his wage is earned, he leaves his statues to be washed away by the next high surging of the tide. The sand-man is often a good artist; let us suppose he were a better one. Let us imagine him endowed with a brain and a hand on a par with those of Praxiteles. None the less we should set his seashore images upon a lower plane of art than the monuments Praxiteles himself hewed out of marble. This we should do instinctively, with no recourse to critical theory; and that man in the multitude who knew the least about art would express this judgment most emphatically. The simple reason would be that the art of the sand-man is lacking in the Intention of Permanence.

The Intention of Permanence, whether it be conscious or subconscious with the artist, is a

necessary factor of the noblest art. Many of
us remember the Court of Honor at the World's
Columbian Exposition, at Chicago fifteen years
ago. The sculpture was good and the architec-
ture better. In chasteness and symmetry of
general design, in spaciousness fittingly re-
strained, in simplicity more decorative than deliberate decoration, those white buildings blooming
into gold and mirrored in a calm lagoon, dazzled
the eye and delighted the æsthetic sense. And yet,
merely because they lacked the Intention of Permanence, they failed to awaken that solemn happy
heartache that we feel in looking upon the tumbled
ruins of some ancient temple. We could never
quite forget that the buildings of the Court of
Honor were fabrics of frame and stucco sprayed
with whitewash, and that the statues were kneaded
out of plaster: they were set there for a year, not
for all time. But there is at Pæstum a crumbled
Doric temple to Poseidon, built in ancient days
to remind the reverent of that incalculable vast-
ness that tosses men we know not whither. It
stands forlorn in a malarious marsh, yet eternally
within hearing of the unsubservient surge. Many
of its massive stones have tottered to the earth;
and irrelevant little birds sing in nests among
the capitals and mock the solemn silence that the
Greeks ordained. But the sacred Intention of
Permanence that filled and thrilled the souls of

those old builders stands triumphant over time; and if only a single devastated column stood to mark their meaning, it would yet be a greater thing than the entire Court of Honor, built only to commemorate the passing of a year.

In all the arts except the acted drama, it is easy even for the layman to distinguish work which is immediate and momentary from work which is permanent and real. It was the turbulent untutored crowd that clamored loudest in demanding that the Dewey Arch should be rendered permanent in marble: it was only the artists and the art-critics who were satisfied by the monument in its ephemeral state of frame and plaster. But in the drama, the layman often finds it difficult to distinguish between a piece intended merely for immediate entertainment and a piece that incorporates the Intention of Permanence. In particular he almost always fails to distinguish between what is really a character and what is merely an acting part. When a dramatist really creates a character, he imagines and projects a human being so truly conceived and so clearly presented that any average man would receive the impression of a living person if he were to read in manuscript the bare lines of the play. But when a playright merely devises an acting part, he does nothing more than indicate to a capable actor the possibility of so comporting himself upon the stage as to convince his audience of humanity in his performance. From the standpoint of criticism, the main difficulty is that the actor's art may frequently obscure the dramatist's lack of art, and *vice versa*, so that a mere acting part may seem, in the hands of a capable actor, a real character, whereas a real character may seem, in the hands of an incapable actor, an indifferent acting part. Rip Van Winkle, for example, was a wonderful acting part for Joseph Jefferson; but it was, from the standpoint of the dramatist, not a character at all, as any one may see who takes the trouble to read the play. Beau Brummel, also, was an acting part rather than a character. And yet the layman, under the immediate spell of the actor's representative art, is tempted in such cases to ignore that the dramatist has merely modeled an image in the sand.

Likewise, on a larger scale, the layman habitually fails to distinguish between a mere theatric entertainment and a genuine drama. A genuine drama always reveals through its imagined struggle of contesting wills some eternal truth of human life, and illuminates some real phases of human character. But a theatric entertainment may present merely a deftly fabricated struggle between puppets, wherein the art of the actor is given momentary exercise. To return to our comparison, a genuine drama is carved out of marble,

and incorporates, consciously or not, the Intention
of Permanence; whereas a mere theatric entertainment may be likened to a group of figures sculp-
tured in the sand.

Those of us who ask much of the contemporary
theatre may be saddened to observe that most of
the current dramatists seem more akin to the sand-
man than to Praxiteles. They have built Courts
of Honor for forty weeks, rather than temples
to Poseidon for eternity. Yet it is futile to condemn an artist who does a lesser thing quite well
because he has not attempted to do a greater
thing which, very probably, he could not do at
all. Criticism, in order to render any practical
service, must be tuned in accordance with the intention of the artist. The important point for
the critic of the sand-man at Coney Island is not
to complain because he is not so enduring an artist
as Praxiteles, but to determine why he is, or
is not, as the case may be, a better artist than
the sand-man at Atlantic City.

X

THE QUALITY OF NEW ENDEAVOR

MANY critics seem to be of the opinion that the work of a new and unknown author deserves and requires less serious consideration than the work of an author of established reputation. There is, however, an important sense in which the very contrary is true. The function of the critic is to help the public to discern and to appreciate what is worthy. The fact of an established reputation affords evidence that the author who enjoys it has already achieved the appreciation of the public and no longer stands in need of the intermediary service of the critic. But every new author advances as an applicant for admission into the ranks of the recognised; and the critic must, whenever possible, assist the public to determine whether the newcomer seems destined by inherent right to enter among the good and faithful servants, or whether he is essentially an outsider seeking to creep or intrude or climb into the fold.

Since everybody knows already who Sir Arthur Wing Pinero is and what may be expected of him, the only question for the critic, in considering a

new play from his practiced pen, is whether or not
the author has succeeded in advancing or maintaining the standard of his earlier and remembered efforts. If, as in *The Wife Without a Smile*, he falls
far below that standard, the critic may condemn the
play, and let the matter go at that. Although the
new piece may be discredited, the author's reputation will suffer no abiding injury from the deep
damnation of its taking off; for the public will
continue to remember the third act of *The Gay
Lord Quex*, and will remain assured that Sir Arthur
Pinero is worth while. But when a play by a
new author comes up for consideration, the public needs to be told not only whether the work
itself has been well or badly done, but also whether
or not the unknown author seems to be inherently
a person of importance, from whom more worthy
works may be expected in the future. The critic
must not only make clear the playwright's present
actual accomplishment, but must also estimate his
promise. An author's first or second play is important mainly — to use Whitman's phrase — as
" an encloser of things to be." The question is
not so much what the author has already done as
what he is likely to do if he is given further hear-
ings. It is in this sense that the work of an unknown playwright requires and deserves more
serious consideration than the work of an acknowl-
edged master. Accomplishment is comparatively

easy to appraise, but to appreciate promise requires forward-looking and far-seeing eyes.

In the real sense, it matters very little whether an author's early plays succeed or fail. The one point that does matter is whether, in either case, the merits and defects are of such a nature as to indicate that the man behind the work is inherently a man worth while. In either failure or success, the sole significant thing is the quality of the endeavor. A young author may fail for the shallow reason that he is insincere; but he may fail even more decisively for the sublime reason that as yet his reach exceeds his grasp. He may succeed because through earnest effort he has done almost well something eminently worth the doing; or he may succeed merely because he has essayed an unimportant and an easy task. Often more hope for an author's future may be founded upon an initial failure than upon an initial success. It is better for a young man to fail in a large and noble effort than to succeed in an effort insignificant and mean. For in labor, as in life, Stevenson's maxim is very often pertinent: — to travel hopefully is frequently a better thing than to arrive.

And in estimating the work of new and unknown authors, it is not nearly so important for the critic to consider their present technical accomplishment as it is for him to consider the sincerity with which they have endeavored to tell the truth about some important phase of human life. Dramatic criticism of an academic cast is of little value either to those who write plays or to those who see them. The man who buys his ticket to the theatre knows little and cares less about the technique of play-making; and for the dramatist himself there are no ten commandments. I have been gradually growing to believe that there is only one commandment for the dramatist, — that he shall tell the truth; and only one fault of which a play is capable,— that, as a whole or in details, it tells a lie. A play is irretrievably bad only when the average theatre-goer — a man, I mean, with no special knowledge of dramatic art — viewing what is done upon the stage and hearing what is said, revolts instinctively against it with a feeling that I may best express in that famous sentence of Assessor Brack's, " People don't do such things." A play that is truthful at all points will never evoke this instinctive dis-approval; a play that tells lies at certain points will lose attention by jangling those who know.

The test of truthfulness is the final test of ex-cellence in drama. In saying this, of course, I do not mean that the best plays are realistic in method, naturalistic in setting, or close to actuality in subject-matter. *The Tempest* is just as true as *The Merry Wives of Windsor*, and *Peter Pan* is just as true as *Ghosts*. I mean merely that the people whom the dramatist has conceived must act and speak at all points consistently with the laws of their imagined existence, and that these laws must be in harmony with the laws of actual life. Whenever people on the stage fail of this consistency with law, a normal theatre-goer will feel instinctively, " Oh, no, he did *not* do that," or, " Those are *not* the words she said." It may safely be predicated that a play is really bad only when the audience does not believe it; for a dramatist is not capable of a single fault, either technical or otherwise, that may not be viewed as one phase or another of untruthfulness.

XI

THE EFFECT OF PLAYS UPON THE PUBLIC

IN the course of his glorious *Song of the Open Road*, Walt Whitman said, " I and mine do not convince by arguments, similes, rhymes; we convince by our presence "; and it has always seemed to me that this remark is peculiarly applicable to dramatists and dramas. The primary purpose of a play is to give a gathered multitude a larger sense of life by evoking its emotions to a consciousness of terror and pity, laughter and love. Its purpose is not primarily to rouse the intellect to thought or call the will to action. In so far as the drama uplifts and edifies the audience, it does so, not by precept or by syllogism, but by emotional suggestion. It teaches not by what it says, but rather by what it deeply and mysteriously is. It convinces not by its arguments, but by its presence.

It follows that those who think about the drama in relation to society at large, and consider as a matter of serious importance the effect of the theatre on the ticket-buying public, should devote profound consideration to that subtle quality of plays which I may call their *tone*. Since the drama convinces less by its arguments than by its presence, less by its intellectual substance than by its emotional suggestion, we have a right to demand that it shall be not only moral but also sweet and healthful and inspiriting.

After witnessing the admirable performance of Mrs. Fiske and the members of her skilfully selected company in Henrik Ibsen's dreary and depressing *Rosmersholm*, I went home and sought solace from a reperusal of an old play, by the buoyant and healthy Thomas Heywood, which is sweetly named *The Fair Maid of the West*. *Rosmersholm* is of all the social plays of Ibsen the least interesting to witness on the stage, because the spectator is left entirely in the dark concerning the character and the motives of Rebecca West until her confession at the close of the third act, and can therefore understand the play only on a second seeing. But except for this important structural defect the drama is a masterpiece of art; and it is surely unnecessary to dwell upon its many merits. On the other hand, *The Fair Maid of the West* is very far from being masterly in art. In structure it is loose and careless; in characterisation it is inconsistent and frequently untrue; in style it is uneven and without distinction. Ibsen, in sheer mastery of dramaturgic means, stands fourth in rank among the world's great dramatists.

Heywood was merely an actor with a gift for telling stories, who flung together upward of two
hundred and twenty plays during the course of
his casual career.   And yet *The Fair Maid of the
West* seemed to me that evening, and seems to me
evermore in retrospect, a nobler work than *Rosmersholm;* for the Norwegian drama gives a dole-
ful exhibition of unnecessary misery, while the
Elizabethan play is fresh and wholesome, and
fragrant with the breath of joy.

Of two plays equally true in content and in
treatment, equally accomplished in structure, in
characterisation, and in style, that one is finally
the better which evokes from the audience the
healthiest and hopefullest emotional response.
This is the reason why *Œdipus King* is a better
play than *Ghosts*.   The two pieces are not dissimilar in subject and are strikingly alike in art.
Each is a terrible presentment of a revolting theme ;
each, like an avalanche, crashes to foredoomed
catastrophe.   But the Greek tragedy is nobler in
tone, because it leaves us a lofty reverence for
the gods, whereas its modern counterpart disgusts
us with the inexorable laws of life,— which are
only the old gods divested of imagined personality.

Slowly but surely we are growing very tired of
dramatists who look upon life with a wry face
instead of with a brave and bracing countenance.
In due time, when (with the help of Mr. Barrie

and other healthy-hearted playmates) we have become again like little children, we shall realise that plays like *As You Like It* are better than all the *Magdas* and the *Hedda Gablers* of the contemporary stage. We shall realise that the way to heal old sores is to let them alone, rather than to rip them open, in the interest (as we vainly fancy) of medical science. We shall remember that the way to help the public is to set before it images of faith and hope and love, rather than images of doubt, despair, and infidelity.

The queer thing about the morbid-minded specialists in fabricated woe is that they believe themselves to be telling the whole truth of human life instead of telling only the worser half of it. They expunge from their records of humanity the very emotions that make life worth the living, and then announce momentously, " Behold reality at last; for this is Life." It is as if, in the midnoon of a god-given day of golden spring, they should hug a black umbrella down about their heads and cry aloud, " Behold, there is no sun!" Shakespeare did that only once,— in *Measure for Measure*. In the deepest of his tragedies, he voiced a grandeur even in obliquity, and hymned the greatness and the glory of the life of man.

Suppose that what looks white in a landscape painting be actually bluish gray. Perhaps it would be best to tell us so; but failing that, it would certainly be better to tell us that it is white than to tell us that it is black.   If our dramatists must idealise at all in representing life, let them idealise upon the positive rather than upon the negative side.   It is nobler to tell us that life is better than it actually is than to tell us that it is worse.   It is nobler to remind us of the joy of living than to remind us of the weariness.   " For to miss the joy is to miss all," as Stevenson remarked; and if the drama is to be of benefit to the public, it should, by its very presence, convey conviction of the truth thus nobly phrased by Matthew Arnold:

<blockquote>
Yet the will is free:
Strong is the Soul, and wise, and beautiful:
The seeds of godlike power are in us still:
Gods are we, Bards, Saints, Heroes, if we will.—
Dumb judges, answer, truth or mockery?
</blockquote>

XII

PLEASANT AND UNPLEASANT PLAYS

THE clever title, *Plays Pleasant and Unpleasant,* which Mr. Bernard Shaw selected for the earliest issue of his dramatic writings, suggests a theme of criticism that Mr. Shaw, in his lengthy prefaces, might profitably have considered if he had not preferred to devote his entire space to a discussion of his own abilities. In explanation of his title, the author stated only that he labeled his first three plays Unpleasant for the reason that " their dramatic power is used to force the spectator to face unpleasant facts." This sentence, of course, is not a definition, since it merely repeats the word to be explained; and therefore, if we wish to find out whether or not an unpleasant play is of any real service in the theatre, we shall have to do some thinking of our own.

It is an axiom that all things in the universe are interesting. The word *interesting* means *capable of awakening some activity of human mind;* and there is no imaginable topic, whether pleasant or unpleasant, which is not, in one way, or another, capable of this effect. But the activities of the human mind are various, and there are therefore several different sorts of interest. The activity of mind awakened by music over waters is very different from that awakened by the binomial theorem. Some things interest the intellect, others the emotions; and it is only things of prime importance that interest them both in equal measure. Now if we compare the interest of pleasant and unpleasant topics, we shall see at once that the activity of mind awakened by the former is more complete than that awakened by the latter. A pleasant topic not only interests the intellect but also elicits a positive response from the emotions; but most unpleasant topics are positively interesting to the intellect alone. In so far as the emotions respond at all to an unpleasant topic, they respond usually with a negative activity. Regarding a thing which is unpleasant, the healthy mind will feel aversion — which is a negative emotion — or else will merely think about it with no feeling whatsoever. But regarding a thing which is pleasant, the mind may be stirred through the entire gamut of positive emotions, rising ultimately to that supreme activity which is Love. This is, of course, the philosophic reason why the thinkers of pleasant thoughts and dreamers of beautiful dreams stand higher in history than those who have thought unpleasantness and have imagined woe.

Returning now to that clever title of Mr. Shaw's,

we may define an unpleasant play as one which
interests the intellect without at the same time
awakening a positive response from the emotions;
and we may define a pleasant play as one which
not only stimulates thought but also elicits sympathy.   To any one who has thoroughly considered the conditions governing theatric art, it should
be evident *a priori* that pleasant plays are better
suited for service in the theatre than unpleasant
plays.   This truth is clearly illustrated by the
facts of Mr. Shaw's career.   As a matter of history, it will be remembered that his vogue in our
theatres has been confined almost entirely to his
pleasant plays.   All four of them have enjoyed a
profitable run; and it is to *Candida*, the best of
his pleasant plays, that, in America at least, he
owes his fame.   Of the three unpleasant plays, *The
Philanderer* has never been produced at all; *Wid-
ower's Houses* has been given only in a series of
special matinées; and *Mrs. Warren's Profession*,
though it was enormously advertised by the fatuous
interference of the police, failed to interest the
public when ultimately it was offered for a run.

Mrs. Warren's Profession is just as interesting
to the thoughtful reader as *Candida*.   It is built
with the same technical efficiency, and written with
the same agility and wit; it is just as sound and
true, and therefore just as moral; and as a criticism, not so much of life as of society, it is in-

dubitably more important.   Why, then, is *Candida*
a better work?   The reason is that the unpleasant
play is interesting merely to the intellect and leaves
the audience cold, whereas the pleasant play is
interesting also to the emotions and stirs the audience to sympathy.   It is possible for the public to
feel sorry for Morell; it is even possible for them
to feel sorry for Marchbanks: but it is absolutely
impossible for them to feel sorry for Mrs. Warren.
The multitude instinctively demands an opportunity to sympathise with the characters presented
in the theatre.   Since the drama is a democratic
art, and the dramatist is not the monarch but the
servant of the public, the voice of the people
should, in this matter of pleasant and unpleasant
plays, be considered the voice of the gods.   This
thesis seems to me axiomatic and unsusceptible of
argument.   Yet since it is continually denied by
the professed " uplifters " of the stage, who persist in looking down upon the public and decrying
the wisdom of the many, it may be necessary to explain the eternal principle upon which it is based.

The truth must be self-evident that theatre-goers
are endowed with a certain inalienable right —
namely, the pursuit of happiness.   The pursuit of
happiness is the most important thing in the world;
because it is nothing less than an endeavor to understand and to appreciate the true, the beautiful,
and the good.   Happiness comes of loving things

which are worthy; a man is happy in proportion to
the number of things which he has learned to love;
and he, of all men, is most happy who loveth best
all things both great and small. For happiness
is the feeling of harmony between a man and his
surroundings, the sense of being at home in the
universe and brotherly toward all worthy things
that are. The pursuit of happiness is simply
a continual endeavor to discover new things that
are worthy, to the end that they may waken love
within us and thereby lure us loftier toward an
ultimate absolute awareness of truth and beauty.
It is in this simple, sane pursuit that people go
to the theatre. The important thing about the
public is that it has a large and longing heart.
That heart demands that sympathy be awakened
in it, and will not be satisfied with merely intellectual discussion of unsympathetic things. It is
therefore the duty, as well as the privilege, of the
dramatist to set before the public incidents which
may awaken sympathy and characters which may
be loved. He is the most important artist in the
theatre who gives the public most to care about.
This is the reason why Joseph Jefferson's *Rip
Van Winkle* must be rated as the greatest creation
of the American stage. The play was shabby
as a work of art, and there was nothing even in
the character to think about; but every perform-

ance of the part left thousands happier, because
their lives had been enriched with a new memory
that made their hearts grow warm with sympathy
and large with love.

238

XIII

THEMES IN THE THEATRE

As the final curtain falls upon the majority of the plays that somehow get themselves presented in the theatres of New York, the critical observer feels tempted to ask the playwright that simple question of young Peterkin in Robert Southey's ballad, *After Blenheim*,—" Now tell us what 't was all about "; and he suffers an uncomfortable feeling that the playwright will be obliged to answer in the words of old Kaspar, " Why, that I cannot tell." The critic has viewed a semblance of a dramatic struggle between puppets on the stage; but what they fought each other for he cannot well make out. And it is evident, in the majority of cases, that the playwright could not tell him if he would, for the reason that the playwright does not know. Not even the author can know what a play is all about when the play isn't about anything. And this, it must be admitted, is precisely what is wrong with the majority of the plays that are shown in our theatres, especially with plays written by American authors. They are not about anything; or, to say the matter more technically, they haven't any theme.

By a theme is meant some eternal principle, or truth, of human life — such a truth as might be stated by a man of philosophic mind in an abstract and general proposition — which the dramatist contrives to convey to his auditors concretely by embodying it in the particular details of his play. These details must be so selected as to represent at every point some phase of the central and informing truth, and no incidents or characters must be shown which are not directly or indirectly representative of the one thing which, in that particular piece, the author has to say. The great plays of the world have all grown endogenously from a single, central idea; or, to vary the figure, they have been spun like spider-webs, filament after filament, out of a central living source. But most of our native playwrights seem seldom to experience this necessary process of the imagination which creates. Instead of working from the inside out, they work from the outside in. They gather up a haphazard handful of theatric situations and try to string them together into a story; they congregate an ill-assorted company of characters and try to achieve a play by letting them talk to each other. Many of our playwrights are endowed with a sense of situation; several of them have a gift for characterisation, or at least for caricature; and most of them can write easy and natural dialogue, especially in slang. But very few of them start out with something to say, as Mr. Moody started out in *The Great Divide* and Mr. Thomas in *The Witching Hour.*

When a play is really about something, it is always possible for the critic to state the theme of it in a single sentence. Thus, the theme of *The Witching Hour* is that every thought is in itself an act, and that therefore thinking has the virtue, and to some extent the power, of action. Every character in the piece was invented to embody some phase of this central proposition, and every incident was devised to represent this abstract truth concretely. Similarly, it would be easy to state in a single sentence the theme of *Le Tartufe,* or of *Othello,* or of *Ghosts.* But who, after seeing four out of five of the American plays that are produced upon Broadway, could possibly tell in a single sentence what they were about? What, for instance — to mention only plays which did not fail — was *Via Wireless* about, or *The Fighting Hope,* or even *The Man from Home?* Each of these was in some ways an interesting entertainment; but each was valueless as drama, because none of them conveyed to its auditors a theme which they might remember and weave into the texture of their lives.

For the only sort of play that permits itself to be remembered is a play that presents a distinct theme to the mind of the observer.   It is ten years since I have seen *Le Tartufe* and six years since last I read it; and yet, since the theme is unforgetable, I could at any moment easily reconstruct the piece by retrospective imagination and summarise the action clearly in a paragraph.   But on the other hand, I should at any time find it impossible to recall with sufficient clearness to summarise them, any of a dozen American plays of the usual type which I had seen within the preceding six months.   Details of incident or of character or of dialogue slip the mind and melt away like smoke into the air.   To have seen a play without a theme is the same, a month or two later, as not to have seen a play at all.   But a piece like *The Second Mrs. Tanqueray*, once seen, can never be forgotten; because the mind clings to the central proposition which the play was built in order to reveal, and from this ineradicable recollection may at any moment proceed by psychologic association to recall the salient concrete features of the action.   To develop a play from a central theme is therefore the sole means by which a dramatist may insure his work against the iniquity of oblivion.   In order that people may afterward remember what he has said, it is necessary for him

to show them clearly and emphatically at the outset why he has undertaken to talk and precisely
what he means to talk about.

Most of our American playwrights, like Juliet
in the balcony scene, speak, yet they say nothing.
They represent facts, but fail to reveal truths.
What they lack is purpose. They collect, instead
of meditating; they invent, instead of wondering;
they are clever, instead of being real. They are
avid of details: they regard the part as greater
than the whole. They deal with outsides and sur-
faces, not with centralities and profundities. They
value acts more than they value the meanings of
acts; they forget that it is in the motive rather
than in the deed that Life is to be looked for.
For Life is a matter of thinking and of feeling;
all act is merely Living, and is significant only
in so far as it reveals the Life that prompted it.
Give us less of Living, more of Life, must ever
be the cry of earnest criticism. Enough of these
mutitudinous, multifarious facts: tell us single,
simple truths. Give us more themes, and fewer
fabrics of shreds and patches.

XIV

THE FUNCTION OF IMAGINATION

WHENEVER the spring comes round and every-thing beneath the sun looks wonderful and new, the habitual theatre-goer, who has attended every legitimate performance throughout the winter season in New York, is moved to lament that there is nothing new behind the footlights. Week after week he has seen the same old puppets pulled mechanically through the same old situations, doing conventional deeds and repeating conventional lines, until at last, as he watches the performance of yet another play, he feels like saying to the author, " But, my dear sir, I have seen and heard all this so many, many times already! " For this spring-weariness of the frequenter of the theatre, the common run of our contemporary playwrights must be held responsible. The main trouble seems to be that, instead of telling us what they think life is like, they tell us what they think a play is like. Their fault is not — to use Hamlet's phrase — that they " imitate humanity so abominably ": it is, rather, that they do not imitate humanity at

233

all. Most of our playwrights, especially the new-comers to the craft, imitate each other. They make plays for the sake of making plays, instead of for the sake of representing life. They draw their inspiration from the little mimic world behind the footlights, rather than from the roaring and tremendous world which takes no thought of the theatre. Their art fails to interpret life, because they care less about life than they care about their art. They are interested in what they are doing, instead of being interested in why they are doing it. "Go to!", they say to themselves, " I will write a play "; and the weary auditor is tempted to murmur the sentence of the cynic Frenchman, "*Je n'en vois pas la nécessité.*"

But now, lest we be led into misapprehension, let us understand clearly that what we desire in the theatre is not new material, but rather a fresh and vital treatment of such material as the playwright finds made to his hand. After a certain philosophic critic had announced the startling thesis that only some thirty odd distinct dramatic situations were conceivable, Goethe and Schiller set themselves the task of tabulation, and ended by deciding that the largest conceivable number was less than twenty. It is a curious paradox of criticism that for new plays old material is best. This statement is supported historically by the fact that all the great Greek dramatists, nearly all of the Elizabethans, Corneille, Racine, Molière, and, to a great extent, the leaders of the drama in the nineteenth century, made their plays deliberately out of narrative materials already familiar to the theatre-going public of their times. The drama, by its very nature, is an art traditional in form and resumptive in its subject-matter. It would be futile, therefore, for us to ask contemporary playwrights to invent new narrative materials. Their fault is not that they deal with what is old, but that they fail to make out of it anything which is new. If, in the long run, they weary us, the reason is not that they are lacking in invention, but that they are lacking in imagination.

That invention and imagination are two very different faculties, that the second is much higher than the first, that invention has seldom been displayed by the very greatest authors, whereas imagination has always been an indispensable characteristic of their work,— these points have all been made clear in a very suggestive essay by Professor Brander Matthews, which is included in his volume entitled *Inquiries and Opinions*. It remains for us to consider somewhat closely what the nature of imagination is. Imagination is nothing more or less than the faculty for *realisation*,— the faculty by which the mind makes real unto itself such materials as are presented to it.

The full significance of this definition may be made clear by a simple illustration.

Suppose that some morning at breakfast you pick up a newspaper and read that a great earthquake has overwhelmed Messina, killing countless thousands and rendering an entire province desolate. You say, " How very terrible! "— after which you go blithely about your business, untroubled, undisturbed. But suppose that your little girl's pet pussy-cat happens to fall out of the fourth-story window. If you chance to be an author and have an article to write that morning, you will find the task of composition heavy. Now, the reason why the death of a single pussycat affects you more than the death of a hundred thousand human beings is merely that you realise the one and do not realise the other. You do not, by the action of imagination, make real unto yourself the disaster at Messina; but when you see your little daughter's face, you at once and easily imagine woe. Similarly, on the largest scale, we go through life realising only a very little part of all that is presented to our minds. Yet, finally, we know of life only so much as we have realised. To use the other word for the same idea,— we know of life only so much as we have imagined. Now, whatever of life we make real unto ourselves by the action of imagination is for us fresh and instant and, in a deep sense, new,— even though the same materials have been realised by millions of human beings before us. It is new because we have made it, and we are different from all our predecessors. Landor imagined Italy, realised it, made it instant and afresh. In the subjective sense, he created Italy, an Italy that had never existed before,— Landor's Italy. Later Browning came, with a new imagination, a new realisation, a new creation,— Browning's Italy. The materials had existed through immemorable centuries; Landor, by imagination, made of them something real; Browning imagined them again and made of them something new. But a Cook's tourist hurrying through Italy is likely, through deficiency of imagination, not to realise an Italy at all. He reviews the same materials that were presented to Landor and to Browning, but he makes nothing out of them. Italy for him is tedious, like a twice-told tale. The trouble is not that the materials are old, but that he lacks the faculty for realising them and thereby making of them something new.

A great many of our contemporary playwrights travel like Cook's tourists through the traditional subject-matter of the theatre. They stop off here and there, at this or that eternal situation; but they do not, by imagination, make it real. Thereby they miss the proper function of the dramatist, which is to imagine some aspect of the perennial struggle between human wills so forcibly as to make us realise it, in the full sense of the word,— realise it as we daily fail to realise the countless struggles we ourselves engage in. The theatre, rightly considered, is not a place in which to escape from the realities of life, but a place in which to seek refuge from the unrealities of actual living in the contemplation of life realised,— life made real by imagination.

The trouble with most ineffective plays is that the fabricated life they set before us is less real than such similar phases of actual life as we have previously realised for ourselves. We are wearied because we have already unconsciously imagined more than the playwright professionally imagines for us. With a great play our experience is the reverse of this. Incidents, characters, motives which we ourselves have never made completely real by imagination are realised for us by the dramatist. Intimations of humanity which in our own minds have lain jumbled fragmentary, like the multitudinous pieces of a shuffled picture-puzzle, are there set orderly before us, so that we see at last the perfect picture. We escape out of chaos into life.

This is the secret of originality: this it is that we desire in the theatre: — not new material, for the old is still the best; but familiar material rendered new by an imagination that informs it with significance and makes it real.

INDEX

INDEX

THE THEATRE

Clayton Hamilton's THEORY OF THE THEATRE. $1.50 net.

Edward Everett Hale, Jr.'s DRAMATISTS OF TO-DAY. Rostand, Hauptmann, Sudermann, Pinero, Shaw, Phillips, Maeterlinck. New Edition with Portraits. $1.50 net.

George Witkowski's GERMAN DRAMA OF THE NINETEENTH CENTURY. $1.00 net.

Calvin Thomas's LIFE AND WORKS OF SCHILLER. $1.50 net.

W. Fraser Rae's LIFE OF RICHARD BRINSLEY SHERIDAN. With portraits. 2 vols. $7.00.

Jerome K. Jerome's ON THE STAGE—AND OFF. Humorous articles on *The Hero, The Stage Child, The Villain* and other stage types. Illustrated. $1.00.

Eva Lathbury's THE SINKING SHIP. A novel of London Theatrical Life. To-day. $1.50.

SHAKESPEARE

Bernhard ten Brink's FIVE LECTURES ON SHAKESPEARE. *The Poet and the Man, The Chronology of Shakepeare's Works, Shakespeare as Dramatist, Shakespeare as Comic Poet, Shakespeare as Tragic Writer.* Index to works mentioned. Translated by Julia Franklin. $1.25 net.

Stopford Brooke's ON TEN PLAYS OF SHAKESPEARE. *Midsummer Night's Dream, Romeo and Juliet, Richard I, Richard II, Merchant of Venice, As You Like It, Macbeth, Coriolanus, Winter's Tale, The Tempest.* $2.25 net.

Stopford Brooke's ON TEN FURTHER PLAYS OF SHAKESPEARE. *Much Ado About Nothing, Twelfth Night, Julius Caesar, Hamlet, Measure for Measure, Othello, King John, King Lear, Henry IV (1, 2); Henry V.* Probable price, $2.25 net. (May.)

John Masefield's SHAKESPEARE. (Home University Library.) 50c. net.

Charlton M. Lewis's THE GENESIS OF HAMLET. $1.25 net.

Felix E. Schelling's ENGLISH LITERATURE DURING THE LIFETIME OF SHAKESPEARE. $2.50 net.

Henry Thew. Stephenson's SHAKESPEARE'S LONDON. Illustrated. $2.00 net.

Stephenson's THE ELIZABETHAN PEOPLE.. Illustrated. $2.00 net.

Postage on net books 8% additional

HENRY HOLT AND COMPANY
PUBLISHERS   NEW YORK

PLAYS

Richard Burton's RAHAB. A drama of the fall of Jericho (in verse.) Illustrated. $1.25 net.

Beulah Marie Dix's ALLISON'S LAD, *The Hundreth Trick, The Weakest Link, The Snare and the Fowler, The Captain of the Gate, The Dark of the Dawn.* One act Martial Interludes. $1.35 net.

Michael Field's CALLIRRHOE; FAIR ROSAMUND. (Dramas in verse.) $1.25.

Henrik Hertz's KING RENE'S DAUGHTER. (A drama in verse.) $1.25.

Kalidasa's SHAKUNTALA. Translated by Prof. A. H. Edgren. $1.50.

Lessing's NATHAN THE WISE. Translated by Ellen Frothingham. $1.50.

Geo. Middleton's EMBERS, with *The Failures, In His House, The Gargoyle, Madonna, The Man Masterful.* $1.35 net.

George Middleton's TRADITION. With *On Bail, Waiting, Their Wife, Mothers, The Cheat of Pity.* Another volume of one act plays of *American Life.* $1.35 net.

Chas. Leonard Moore's THE BANQUET OF PALACIOS. A comedy of South America. To-day. $1.00.

Martin Schutze's HERO AND LEANDER. A tragedy in verse. $1.25 net.

Martin Schutze's JUDITH. A tragedy in verse $1.25 net.

Margaret L. Woods' THE PRINCESS OF HANOVER. An historical tragedy in verse. $1.50.

***For a large number of plays in Foreign Languages, see the publishers' FOREIGN LANGUAGE CATALOG.

PLAYS FOR YOUNG FOLKS

Constance D'Arcy Mackay's PATRIOTIC PLAYS AND PAGE-ANTS, *Pageant of Patriotism, Hawthorne Pageant.* Parts of the first pageant can be given as one act plays. $1.35 net.

C. D'A. Mackay's THE HOUSE OF THE HEART with *The Enchanted Garden, A Little Pilgrim's Progress, A Pageant of Hours, On Christmas Eve, The Elf Child, The Princess and the Pixies,* etc. $1.10 net.

C. D'A. Mackay's THE SILVER THREAD and other Folk Plays, including *The Forest Spring, Troll Magic, The Three Wishes, Siegfried, The Snow Witch,* etc. $1.10 net.

*** For a number of French and German plays for young folk, see also the publishers' FOREIGN LANGUAGE CATALOG.

*Postage on net books 8% additional.

HENRY HOLT AND COMPANY
34 WEST 33d STREET   NEW YORK

BEULAH MARIE DIX'S
ALLISON'S LAD AND OTHER MARTIAL
INTERLUDES

By the co-author of the play, "The Road to Yesterday," and
author of the novels, "The Making of Christopher Ferring-
ham," "Blount of Breckenlow," etc. 12mo. $1.35 net; by
mail, $1.45.

*Allison's Lad, The Hundredth Trick, The Weakest Link,
The Snare and the Fowler, The Captain of the Gate, The
Dark of the Dawn.*

These one-act plays, despite their impressiveness, are perfectly practicable for performance by clever amateurs; at the
same time they make decidedly interesting reading.

Six stirring war episodes. Five of them occur at night,
and most of them in the dread pause before some mighty
conflict. Three are placed in Cromwellian days (two in Ire-
land and one in England), one is at the close of the French
Revolution, another at the time of the Hundred Years' War,
and the last during the Thirty Years' War. The author has
most ingeniously managed to give the feeling of big events,
though employing but few players. The emotional grip is
strong, even tragic.

Courage, vengeance, devotion, and tenderness to the weak,
are among the emotions effectively displayed.

" The technical mastery of Miss Dix is great, but her spiritual mastery
is greater. For this book lives in memory, and the spirit of its
teachings is, in a most intimate sense, the spirit of its teacher. . . .
Noble passion holding the balance between life and death is the motif
sharply outlined and vigorously portrayed. In each interlude the author
has seized upon a vital situation and has massed all her forces so as
to enhance its significance."—*Boston Transcript.* (Entire notice on application to the publishers.)

" Highly dramatic episodes, treated with skill and art . . . a high
pitch of emotion."—*New York Sun.*

" Complete and intense tragedies well plotted and well sustained, in
dignified dialogue of persons of the drama distinctly differentiated."—
Hartford Courant.

" It is a pleasure to say, without reservation, that the half dozen
plays before us are finely true, strong, telling examples of dramatic
art. . . . Sure to find their way speedily to the stage, justifying
themselves there, even as they justify themselves at a reading as pieces
of literature."—*The Bellman.*

HENRY HOLT AND COMPANY
PUBLISHERS   **NEW YORK**

TWO POETIC DRAMAS

By MARTIN SCHÜTZE

JUDITH
$1.25 net ; by mail $1.33.

"Mr. Schutze has given us a new Holofernes, and in doing this he has very greatly intensified the tragic situation. . . . A well-developed tragical motif . . . that wonderful moment of climax. . . . The tragic integrity of the character of Judith is maintained. . . . The details of the drama are well carried out. . . . Mr. Schutze has not only been able to change traditional elements in the old story and yet render his version strong and convincing, but he has also given us a memorable addition to the old Judith legend."
—*Boston Transcript.*

"Among the best modern achievements. . . . Developed with extraordinary power, both in the structure of the drama and in the verse, rich in beautiful imagery and in the power and dignity which the theme and the time demand. The author has shown a wonderful mastery of his materials and has succeeded admirably in making his characters live against the background of the Judean hills."—*Philadelphia Ledger.*

"Well within the unities and purposes of true tragedy, . . . an atmosphere at once classic and modern."—*Chicago Tribune.*

"A picture is given of the religious austerity of the Jews, and much is made of their national jealousy. Holofernes is a man of princely character. . . . This devotion of Judith to the human excellence which she discerned in Holofernes gives an unexpected turn to the narrative and fits it better for modern interpretation."—*Springfield Republican.*

"A poetic psychological study that at worst is interesting and at best is keenly dramatic. . . . In the multitudinous cast there are several excellent bits for good actors. . . . Plenty of characters and telling situations."—*New York Dramatic Mirror.*

HERO AND LEANDER
$1.25 net ; by mail $1.33.

"Perhaps the fullest and strongest drama that has ever been written about these lovers."—*Chicago Record-Herald.*

"The consecration of Hero in the Temple of Venus, the apparition of Leander, his encounter with the temple guards, the episodes attending Hero's surrender, and the storm with its tragic outcome are all valuable theatrical incidents . . . a capable, dignified, and interesting composition which would be a credit to any theatre producing it."—*Nation.*

"Vivid scenes. . . . The death of Hero is an opportunity seized by the author for more than usually effective lines ; and the closing scene sustains well the tragic distinction of the climax."—*Hartford Courant.*

"Unusual strength of construction and poetic expression."—*Providence Journal.*

"Here is, indeed, a beautiful talent of the greatest promise, a soaring fancy, poesy of thought and imagination as well as of form, and sound classic scholarship."—*Independent.*

HENRY HOLT AND COMPANY

PUBLISHERS   **NEW YORK**

(OVER)